Years 6–10 Literacy
FOR STUDENTS

Years 6–10 Literacy FOR STUDENTS

by Wendy M Anderson
Geraldine Woods
Lesley J Ward
Christopher Danielson, PhD
Tracey Wood, MEd

Made by the people who make the DUMMIES books!
A Wiley Brand

Years 6–10 Literacy for Students®

Published by
Wiley Publishing Australia Pty Ltd
42 McDougall Street
Milton, Qld 4064
www.dummies.com

Copyright © 2016 Wiley Publishing Australia Pty Ltd

The moral rights of the authors have been asserted.

National Library of Australia
Cataloguing-in-Publication data:

Author:	Wendy M Anderson
Contributors:	Geraldine Woods, Lesley J Ward, Christopher Danielson, Tracey Wood
Title:	Years 6–10 Literacy for Students
ISBN:	9780730326762 (pbk.)
	9780730326755 (ebook)
Series:	For Dummies
Notes:	Includes index.
Subjects:	Literacy—Study and teaching (Secondary)—Australia.
	English language—Study and teaching (Secondary)—Australia.
	English language—Australia—Textbooks.
	English language—Problems, exercises, etc.
Dewey Number:	428.00712

Cover: Wiley Creative Services

Typeset by diacriTech, Chennai, India

Printed in Australia by
Ligare Book Printer

10 9 8 7 6 5 4 3 2 1

Contents at a Glance

Table of Contents

Introduction

. . . .

*L*iteracy and English grammar can be tricky, and they make lots of people nervous. Chances are, you're reading this now because you're one of those people. This can be stressful and make you feel self-conscious. And it's worse if everyone else seems to understand, and knows how to use perfect grammar (even in text messages) or has amazing spelling and vocabulary abilities.

Happily, however, literacy and English grammar are easier than you may think. You don't have to memorise all of the technical terms, and you're likely to find that you already know a lot of it anyway. In this book, we tell you the tricks of the trade, and the strategies that help you make the right decision when you're facing such grammatical dilemmas as how to choose between *I* and *me*, whether to say *had gone* or *went*, or if you should put the apostrophe in *its*. And we help you with spelling demons and comprehension clunkers.

Importantly, we explain *what* you're supposed to do, tell you *why* a particular way of doing things is correct or incorrect, and even show you *how* to revise your sentences if your grammar checker puts a squiggly green line under some part of your sentence. We help you polish your vocabulary and improve your writing, and provide tips on when a particular way of spelling a word is correct (something your grammar checker can't always help you with). When you understand the reason for a particular choice, you'll pick the correct option automatically.

About This Book

In this book, we concentrate on the common errors. We tell you what's what in the sentence, in logical, everyday English, not in obscure terminology. You don't have to read the chapters in order, but you can. And you don't have to read the whole book. Just browse through the table of contents and look for things that have always troubled you. For example, if you know that verbs are your downfall, check out Chapters 2 and 3 for the basics. Chapter 12 covers vocabulary and writing techniques such as similes and metaphors. You decide what you need to focus on.

Most chapters in this book introduce some basic ideas and then show you how to choose the correct sentence when faced with two or three choices. If we define a term — *linking verbs*, for example — we show you a practical situation in which identifying a linking verb helps you pick the right pronoun. The examples are clearly displayed in the text so that you can find them easily. One good way to determine whether or not you need to read a particular section is to have a go at the 'Have a Go' tasks that are sprinkled around most chapters. If you get the right answer, you probably don't need to read that section. If you're stumped, however, backtrack and read the chapter.

Throughout the book, we've used grey text boxes — the sidebars — for information that you may find interesting but isn't required for your understanding of the subject. Feel free to flick straight past them.

Foolish Assumptions

We wrote this book with a specific person in mind. We assume that you, the reader, already speak English (although you may have learned it as a foreign language) and that you want to speak and write it better. We also assume that you have better things to do than worry about *who* and *whom*. You want to speak and write well, but you don't want to go on to get a doctorate in English grammar in a few years' time. (Smart move. Doctorates in English don't move you very far up the salary scale.)

This book is for you if you aspire to

- ✔ Improving your skills in grammar, punctuation, spelling, vocabulary and reading comprehension.
- ✔ Transferring these improvements to your writing and reading, both for school purposes and for life.
- ✔ Preparing for the NAPLAN tests.

Icons Used in This Book

Throughout this book you can find useful icons to help you note specific types of information. Here's what each icon means:

Have you ever been confused by the message your grammar checker gives you when it puts a wiggly line under a possible problem and asks you to 'consider revising' some part of your sentence? Your days of confusion end here. This little fellow appears at the same points that a wiggly line would appear, and the information alongside it tells you exactly how to revise those troublesome sentences.

Think you know how to find the subject in a sentence, identify a pronoun or spell a tricky word? Have a go at these exercises, located throughout this book, to find out what you know and what you may want to learn.

 Wherever you see this icon, you'll find helpful strategies for understanding the structure of the sentence, choosing the correct word form or improving your writing.

 Not every grammar and vocabulary trick has a built-in trap, but some do. This icon tells you how to avoid common mistakes as you unravel a sentence.

Where to Go From Here

Now that you know what's what and where it is, it's time to get started. Pick any chapter or specific area you need more help with and jump in. Before you do, however, one last word. Actually, two last words. *Trust yourself.* You already know a lot. You'd be amazed how much grammar, vocabulary and spelling awareness can be absorbed by osmosis from day-to-day language. If you're a native speaker, you've communicated in English all of your life, including the years before you set foot in school and saw your first textbook. If English is an acquired language for you, you've probably already learned a fair amount of vocabulary and grammar, even if you don't know the technical terms. So take heart. Browse through the table of contents, have a go at a few tasks and dip a toe into the sea of English literacy and grammar. The water's fine.

Part I
Understanding Verbs and Sentences

getting started with
Years 6–10 Literacy for

STUDENTS

In this part . . .

- Understand the difference between formal and informal English — and when each is appropriate.
- Work out the building blocks of a sentence and why verbs are so important.
- Identify the verb in a sentence — and know what to do with it once you've found it.
- Discover the subject in a sentence and how to match subjects and verbs so they get along.
- Match pronouns with their correct noun, and avoid vague (or just plain incorrect) pronoun use.

Chapter 1

Why is Grammar Important?

Good communication and good grammar go hand in hand. The very point of using language is to express and exchange ideas in a way that conveys them clearly, with as few misunderstandings as possible. Sure, an occasional 'Oh, you know what I mean' is not going to stop the world from turning or upset your friends and family, but if you need to impress somebody, you need your communication to be accurate. If you want your essay to shine, your history presentation to captivate or (in a few years' time, perhaps) your application for that part-time job to be successful, using good grammar will help you to achieve these things.

Of course, you probably already have pretty good grammar. Most people learn the basics of language use as if by osmosis, picking it up without necessarily understanding the rules. After all, you're likely to have been talking almost all of your life and have probably forgotten when and how you first learned to read and write. But the fact that you have this book in your hands means that you have decided that improving your English grade and learning *better* language skills and grammar is a valuable strategy. Yay you! This book will help you become a better communicator.

In this chapter, we look closely at what constitutes proper grammar and how language use can change, depending on the situation. We also take a trip back in time to revisit probably the first thing you were taught about grammar as we consider the very basic unit of communication: the word.

You may be reading this book for a number of reasons. Perhaps you're hoping to impress your English teacher or hoping for a good NAPLAN score. If English was your first language, you probably learnt English comprehension and grammar by osmosis, by hearing what others say, which, all too often, means absorbing a fair chunk of incorrect grammar along with the correct bits. If English wasn't your first language, you've likely similarly picked up correct (and incorrect) vocabulary and grammar as you've learnt the language.

Whatever your ultimate goal is, you seem to have decided that learning better grammar is a valuable strategy. Good for you! In this chapter, we look a little more closely at why good grammar is so important. We also look at how the definition of *better grammar* changes according to your situation, purpose and audience. And we provide some tips for parents helping you as you build your skills.

Functioning with Good Grammar

Rightly or wrongly, your audience or readers judge you by the words you use and the way you string them together. Listen to the speech of the people in movies. An uneducated character sounds different from someone with five diplomas on the wall. The dialogue reflects reality: educated people follow certain rules when they speak and write. In fact, people who use language according to formal grammar rules are said to be speaking *properly*. After you leave school, if you want to present yourself as an educated person, you'll have to follow those rules too.

Actually, several different types of grammar exist, including *historical* (how language has changed through the centuries) and *comparative* (comparing languages). Some English teachers love to complicate things. But don't worry; we love to keep things simple. In this book, we use the best bits of the two easiest, most familiar ways of presenting the rules of grammar to come up with what's proper.

Descriptive grammar gives names to things — the parts of speech, or word groups, and parts of a sentence. When you learn descriptive grammar, you understand what every word *is* (its part of speech) and what every word *does* (its function in the sentence). Learning some grammar terms has a couple of important advantages — to be clear about *why* a particular word or phrase is correct or incorrect, and to be able to understand the explanations and advice given by your computer's grammar checker or in a dictionary or style guide.

Functional grammar tells you how words behave when they're doing their jobs properly. It guides you to the right expression — the one that fits what you're trying to say — by ensuring that the sentence is put together correctly. When you're agonising over whether to say *I* or *me*, you're solving a problem of functional grammar. Most of the grammar we use in this book is functional grammar.

So here's the formula for better grammar: a little descriptive grammar plus a lot of functional grammar. Better grammar equals better self-expression. And better self-expression equals improved self-confidence. And with improved self-confidence, anything is possible. The news is all good!

Choosing Levels of English

So, using good grammar clearly sounds like a great idea, but you may not always need to use standard English because the language of choice depends on your situation. Here's what we mean. Imagine you're out with your friends and realise you're hungry. How would you invite them back to your house for lunch?

Would you care to accompany me home for lunch?

Wanna come to mine for a bite?

Different levels of English are used in everyday life. We call the first example *formal English*, and the second example *informal English*. If you're like most people, you switch between levels of English without even thinking about it. You choose the most suitable level of language depending on where you are, what's going on and who your audience is.

Impressing with formal English

Formal English shows that you've trotted out your best behaviour in someone's honour. You may use formal English when you have less power, importance and/or status than the other person in the conversation. Think of formal English as English on its best behaviour and wearing a business suit. If you're in a situation where you want to look your best, or in which you're being judged, use formal English.

Situations and types of writing that call for formal English include

✔ Authoritative reference books

✔ Business letters and emails (from individuals to businesses, as well as from or between businesses)

✔ Homework

✔ Important conversations such as job interviews, university interviews, sessions with teachers in which you explain that it wasn't you who did what they think you did, that sort of thing

✔ Letters to government officials

✔ Notes or letters to teachers

✔ Reports

✔ Speeches, presentations and formal oral reports

Chances are formal English is the one that gives you the most trouble. In fact, it's probably why you bought this book. So, the grammar lessons you'll find here deal with how to handle formal English, because that's where the rewards for knowledge are greatest.

Chatting in informal English

Informal English is casual and often strays from the rules, even breaking some. It's the tone of most everyday speech, especially between equals. In informal English we take short cuts and combine words: *let's, we've, I'll.* Using informal English is fine for conversations, emails to friends or a note to your brother, but not for writing an essay or a presentation.

In the written form, informal English also relaxes the punctuation rules. Sentences run together, dashes connect all sorts of things, and half-sentences pop up regularly. This book is in conversational English because we like to think we're chatting with you, the reader, not teaching grammar in a classroom. Think of informal English as being like English in jeans and a T-shirt: Perfectly comfortable and presentable, but not suitable as corporate attire.

Specifically, informal English is appropriate in these situations:

✔ Comments made on public internet sites

✔ Communication (including by email or snail mail) with your extended personal community of family, friends and acquaintances

✔ Incidental conversations (but not in writing) with teachers and other school staff

✔ Fiction and memoir writing

Labelling Words

No doubt you've been in the frustrating position of having to try to decode what someone is trying to tell you about 'What's-her-name ... You know ... She used to teach that class ... She has a sort of large thingamabob'. Without the right words, the correct labels, you cannot understand the message. The same is true when talking about language or, more specifically, about grammar. You don't need to be an English teacher or a walking dictionary, but you do need to understand the key terms so that we can communicate efficiently. So we're going to introduce you to (or just reacquaint you with) some of the most important grammar terms, starting with the labels used for *word classes* or *parts of speech*. Understanding these is the first step to better grammar.

Nouns

We use nouns to provide a name or label. We have nouns for people (*lawyer, Vincent*); places (*beach, Monkey Mia*); objects (*pen, bird*); feelings (*happiness, boredom*); concepts (*accountability, freedom*); qualities (*bravery, intelligence*); ideas (*imagination, notion*); and activities (*cricket, dancing, shopping*). Nouns are rarely troublemakers, but in Chapter 6 we take a peek at how they work in descriptions, while in Chapter 9 the connection between nouns and capital letters is made clear.

Pronouns

The name *pronoun* makes this part of speech sound either like a highly skilled, professional (pro) noun, or a class of word that is totally in favour of (pro) nouns. While both are possible, neither is entirely correct. A *pronoun* is a word that can be used in the place of a *noun*. (See how handy it is to have basic grammar vocabulary at your fingertips? Some parts of speech are defined according to their relationship to other word classes.) Chapter 5 explains how to peak with pronouns, but, in the meantime, here's an example of how *pronouns* substitute for *nouns* to minimise tedious repetition in communication:

- ✔ **With nouns (yawn):** If *Kelly* wants to bring *Kelly's* friend, *Kelly* is welcome to do so.
- ✔ **With pronouns:** If Kelly wants to bring *her* friend, *she* is welcome to do so.
- ✔ **Also with pronouns:** If *you* want to bring *your* friend, *you* are welcome to do so.

Verbs

If you delve back into a dark corner of your brain, you can probably recall chanting the definition, 'A verb is a doing word'. Powering your language is exactly what the verb is 'doing'. Verbs refer to actions (*eat, write, take*), conditions (*seem, appear, become*) or states of being (*am, is, are*). They're also the key to understanding when a sentence is grammatically correct, so these guys deserve close attention. To locate a verb in a sentence, you need to ask yourself these questions: *What's happening? What is?* The word that provides the answer is the *verb*.

Because they change their form and attach to other verbs or other parts of speech to change their meaning, verbs can be tricky. But verbs have power, and understanding how they work is probably the most essential of all grammar essentials. Chapters 2 and 3 take you further into the world of verbs.

Adjectives

When we add more information to a *noun* or *pronoun*, the word we use is called an *adjective*. Adjectives add to, describe or modify nouns and pronouns. They can be found lurking either in front of a noun or pronoun, or after a special kind of *verb* called a *linking verb* (you can read all about verbs in Chapter 2). Because adjectives add colour and detail to our language, they're worth careful consideration, so Chapter 6 provides ample advice but, basically, adjectives work like this:

Before a noun: The *sneaky* adjective attaches itself to the *unsuspecting* noun.

Before a pronoun: The noun is the *unsuspecting* one.

After a linking verb: The adjective is *sneaky* and the noun is *unsuspecting*.

Adverbs

Another of those grammar chants you may have learned at one stage goes like this: 'An adverb adds meaning to a verb by telling us how, when, where or why a thing is done'. While that's true, it's only part of the adverb story. Adverbs can also be used to modify adjectives or even other adverbs. Another thing you may vaguely remember is that adverbs often end with *-ly*. True. But not all adverbs end with those letters, and *lovely* is an adjective.

So, reading Chapter 6 will help you to master adverbs and to write so that your descriptions say precisely what you mean. Here are some adverbs at work:

- ✔ **With a verb:** The sun shines *brightly*.
- ✔ **With an adjective:** The day feels *unbearably hot*.
- ✔ **With another adverb:** The sea glistens *most enticingly*.

Determiners

There was once a word class for just three words: *a, the, an*. They formed the word group called *articles*. But what makes those three little words so special? Well ... Ummm ... Nothing really. They do the same job as lots of other words. So, we now include articles in a word class called *determiners*. A raft of words that also fit into other classes work extra shifts as determiners. Like articles, determiners go in front of a noun or a group of words that's doing the work of a noun, and tell you how specific or otherwise something is.

Common determiners are words such as *the, both, every, my, his, our, this, that, these, those, each, ten*. As you can no doubt see, some of those words look suspiciously like other parts of speech — pronouns, for example (*my, his, our*), or adjectives (*each, both, ten*). Different grammar books or teachers may even refer to them as such. What you need to know is that we prefer the simplest, most logical way of explaining language, so throughout this book, we'll stick with the label *determiner*.

Prepositions

If all the parts of speech were to form a sporting team, Preposition would be the easy-going one who fills in wherever and whenever required. During the game, Preposition would consistently pass the ball to Noun or Pronoun so they can score the points. *Prepositions* are unassuming but important contributors to the language game.

Prepositions show a relationship between a noun and another word. We can relate the two nouns 'book' and 'wombat' by using various prepositions to express different ideas. The book could be *about* the wombat, *beside* the wombat or maybe *behind* the wombat. This would mean that the wombat was *in* the book, *near* the book and *in front of* the book.

Prepositions (the words in italics in the previous paragraph) come in front of a noun or group of words acting as a noun. That's why they're called *pre + positions*. We provide more details on how prepositions work in Chapter 4.

Conjunctions

The fact that the label *conjunction* contains the word *junction* is no coincidence. Just as a junction connects two or more roads, so a *conjunction* connects two or more words. Common joining words are *and*, *but*, *because*, *so*, *or*. That's pretty straightforward, but conjunctions come in several varieties, which is important to understand when you need to connect whole ideas rather than just individual words. Chapter 4 shows you how important they are for connecting ideas in a logical way.

Articles

As mentioned in the 'Determiners' section (earlier in this chapter), just three little words make up the articles. They hardly seem worthy of their own part of speech. Just like adjectives, articles are words that modify nouns and noun equivalents. They are those little words — *a, an, the* — that sit in front of nouns. In meaning, *the* is usually more specific than *an* or *a*.

> *The* teacher wants *the* answer, and soon.

Here, *the teacher* means one teacher in particular. Lots of teachers are in the world, but the sentence is referring to the one who marks your tests. And she wants *the* answer. Not any old answer, but the right answer.

> The teacher wants *an* answer, and you'd better be quick about it.

We're still talking about one particular teacher, but this time we're told that she wants *an* answer. She's been waiting for a while, so you'd better come up with some kind of answer ASAP.

The is called the *definite* article (used definitely for just one specific thing). *A* and *an* are called *indefinite* articles (used for no single thing in particular).

To sum up: Use *the* when you're speaking specifically and *an* or *a* when you're speaking more generally.

So what's the difference between *a* and *an*? *A apple? An book? A* precedes words that begin with consonant sounds (all the letters except *a, e, i, o* and *u*). *An* precedes words beginning with the vowel sounds *a, e, i* and *o*. The letter *u* is a special case. If the letter sounds like *you*, choose *a* (*a university*, for example). If the letter sounds like someone kicked you in the stomach — *uh* — choose *an* (as in *it was an understandable mistake*).

Another special case is the letter *h*. If the word starts with a hard *h* sound (as in *horse*) choose *a*. If the word starts with a silent letter *h* (as in *hour*), choose *an*.

Turning to Reference Books for Help

Even with all the information and tips we provide in this book, you may still need some extra help to make sure you're using the best word for your audience and purpose when you write. Two very useful reference tools are the dictionary and the thesaurus.

Digging into dictionaries

What can a dictionary tell you about a word? Well, it not only gives you the meaning or meanings, but also tells you how to pronounce the word and whether the word is a noun or an adjective. A dictionary can also provide alternative words — which can save you time in not needing to refer to a thesaurus. Figure 1-1 shows some sample pages from the *Macquarie School Dictionary*, which can help you identify the special features of this useful resource.

Using the sample dictionary pages shown in Figure 1-1, answer the following questions.

Which headword comes after *Balmain bug*?

Is the headword *balmy* (a) a noun (b) an adjective or (c) a verb?

What is the definition or meaning of the headword *banal*?

What are some alternative words for *band²*?

What is the origin or word history of the word *bare*?

What word is the opposite of *ban*?

What is the adjective from *bacteria*?

A guide to the Macquarie School Dictionary

Guideword: bacteria — billabong

bacteria
plural noun microscopic living bodies with one cell, which multiply by dividing themselves in two and which can cause disease and decay
Noun forms: The singular is **bacterium**.
Word building: **bacterial** *adjective*
Word history: Neo-Latin, from Greek word meaning 'little stick'

You will sometimes see **bacteria** used with a singular verb. Some people feel that this is not acceptable as **bacteria** is the plural form of **bacterium**.
Look up **germ / bacterium / virus**.

ballistic
adjective **1** having to do with ballistics
phrase **2 go ballistic,** *Colloquial* to become extremely angry: *Dad will go ballistic when he sees this mess.*

Balmain bug
noun an edible flattened crustacean first discovered in Port Jackson (Sydney Harbour), similar to the Moreton Bay bug
Word history: named after *Balmain*, a suburb of Sydney, New South Wales

balmy (bah-mee)
adjective fine or pleasant: *In the balmy spring weather they often sit outdoors.* (*fair, mild, sunny, temperate*)
Adjective forms: **balmier, balmiest**

ban
verb to bar or forbid: *Our teacher banned chewing gum from the classroom.* (*censor, disqualify, exclude, outlaw, prevent*)
Word use: The opposite of this is **allow**.
Verb forms: I **banned**, I have **banned**, I am **banning**
Word history: Middle English, from Scandinavian

banal (buh-nahl, bay-nuhl)
adjective ordinary and unoriginal: *The TV film was so banal that we turned it off.* (*clichéd, commonplace, hackneyed, trite, unimaginative*)
Word building: **banality** *noun*
Word history: French, from Germanic word meaning 'proclamation'

band[1]
noun **1** a group of people acting together: *a band of outlaws* (*bunch, crowd, gang, huddle, troop*) **2** a group of musicians: *a rock band / a brass band* **3** to join in a group: *to band together to protect the environment*
Word history: French, from Germanic

band[2]
noun **1** a strip of material for tying, binding or decorating: *a hat band / a rubber band* **2** a narrow strip that contrasts with its surroundings: *a band of red paint* (*line, stripe*) **3** *Mining* a layer of stone containing ore or a similar valuable material, such as opal (*deposit, seam, stratum, vein*) **4** *Radio* a defined or specified range of frequencies: *The radio station I listen to is part of the FM band.*
Word history: Middle English, from French

bare
adjective **1** uncovered or naked: *bare walls / bare knees* (*bald, exposed, nude, unclad*) **2** plain or simple: *the bare truth* (*basic, essential, stark, unadorned*)
verb **3** to expose or uncover: *The fierce dog began to bare its teeth.*
Word building: **bareness** *noun*
Word history: Old English *baer*

bare / bear
Don't confuse **bare** with **bear**, which is a large furry mammal. It can also mean 'to carry or support something':
I can't bear your weight any longer.

be
The most common verb in English is the verb **to be**. It appears in several different forms, and some of them look quite different from **be**:

Present	Past
(I) am	(I, he, she, it) was
(we, you, they) are	(we, you, they) were
(he, she, it) is	
being (present participle)	been (past participle)

The verb **to be** can act on its own, or together with other verbs. That is, it can be a main verb or an auxiliary verb:
She is a doctor. (main verb)
They have hurt last week. (main verb)
He was walking to the beach. (auxiliary verb)
You are coming on Friday. (auxiliary verb)
The present and past forms, except for **am**, often form contractions with the word **not**. For example:

is not	becomes	isn't
are not	becomes	aren't
was not	becomes	wasn't
were not	becomes	weren't

You shouldn't contract **am not** to **amn't**. Instead, **am** contracts with **I** to become **I'm not**. Note that you should avoid using **ain't** unless you're writing down ungrammatical speech or dialogue.

bilby
noun a small bandicoot with big rabbit-like ears
Noun forms: The plural is **bilbies**.
Word history: from Yuwaalaraay, an Australian Aboriginal language from the Lightning Ridge region

billabong
noun Australian a waterhole which used to be part of a river
Word history: from Wiradjuri, an Australian Aboriginal language of the Murrumbidgee-Lachlan region. The word *billa* meant 'river' and the ending -*bong* meant 'happening only after rain'. In the Aboriginal language this was the name of what the settlers called the Bell River, but it came to be used more widely for waterholes, particularly those that seemed to be separated from a flowing river.

Callout labels (left): Guideword · Headword · Word building—other members of the headword's family · Usage notes in shaded entries · Idiomatic phrase · Label telling you how the phrase is used · Part of speech · Word use telling you something interesting about the word · Adjective forms—those not formed by simply adding -er or -est, or by using the words more or most · How to say the word—see the pronunciation key on page v · Verb forms giving you other tenses of the verb · Words that are spelt the same but have different histories · Change of part of speech · Label telling you this subject area of the word (as) used in a particular definition

Callout labels (right): Guideword · Thesaurus entries · A sentence or phrase including the headword, showing you how it is used in context · Grammar notes in shaded entries · Usage notes in shaded entries · Word history telling you where the word came from · Interesting word histories given in shaded notes

Figure 1-1: Taking advantage of all the features in a dictionary.

Thumbing through the thesaurus

A thesaurus is essentially a place for finding words, and works in an opposite way to a dictionary. Whereas a dictionary defines the different meanings of words, a thesaurus groups words with similar meanings together.

The words grouped together in a thesaurus have similar meanings, but no two words in the English language have exactly the same meaning — otherwise, we would have no need for two words!

All thesauruses include an explanation in the front of how they are organised, so make sure you read this explanation before proceeding.

Say you want to find another word for *big* and so look it up in a thesaurus. The word you choose will depend on factors such as audience and purpose. If you were writing advertising copy for a new breakfast cereal, for example, you might choose *family sized* to describe the size of the packet. If you were writing a new national anthem, you might choose *bounteous* to describe the size of Australia's natural riches. Would you use *family sized* to describe Australia's natural riches, or *bounteous* to describe the size of the cereal packet? Why not?

What Parents Can Do to Help

As parents see their children struggling with their English homework, or struggling to improve their marks in English, many want to offer some help and guidance. The following sections show you how to provide this help — without taking over.

Helping your child with homework (without doing the work yourself)

Whatever the standards may be — based on the Australian Curriculum or anything else — most children will be frustrated with a homework assignment from time to time. The advice to you, the parent, doesn't change.

What may have changed since you went to school is the ways children are expected to work on their homework. Teachers may ask their students to practise something they worked on in class, but it may look unfamiliar to you. Productive ways of helping children with their homework are the same, though.

Researchers have found that the human mind is surprisingly lazy. If it can get something done without thinking hard, it will. This research is no surprise to someone who has witnessed a typical 10-year-old child eager to get through her English homework so that she can go outside and play. 'Is this the right meaning for *homophone*?' she asks, hopefully. 'Is it right now? What about this?' This routine can quickly devolve into a guessing game rather than a chance to learn anything useful.

An important function of homework is what teachers call *formative assessment*, which means learning what students understand while they're still studying it. A classroom full of correct homework papers can signal to a teacher that everyone understands and it's time to move on. Now imagine if those correct homework papers were the result of parents (or tutors or older siblings) walking these children through the steps of the homework problems. It could mislead the teacher. It's much better to write a note explaining what the student is struggling with (or to let your child submit some incorrect or incomplete problems) than to let the teacher think that your child understands something that he doesn't.

Don't do the homework for your child. Help your child clarify his thinking and identify what he knows and doesn't know. Monitor the difficulty level to make sure your child has interesting and challenging work, but not work that is far beyond his present abilities. Keep in touch with his teacher if things are out of balance so that you can work together for your child's benefit.

In the heat of the moment, though, you can easily lose sight of the big picture. So here are three simple tips for productive involvement with English homework and for getting students to think instead of guess and so to learn something rather than just stumble onto a right answer:

- ✔ **Ask, 'How do you know?'** This question forces students to think about their own thinking, which is an important part of making that thinking better. Ask this question frequently. Question right and wrong answers. Also keep in mind that this question has many variations. 'How do you know this is right?', 'How did you know that was wrong?', 'How did you know to do that?', and so on.

- ✔ **Wait for a response.** Ten or 15 seconds seems like a long time to sit silently when you know the correct spelling or word to choose, but it's not long at all to the person trying to figure the answer out. What goes on in the silent time between asking a question and getting an answer is thinking. One of the most important findings in educational research is that increased *wait time* — the time between a teacher asking a question and the next time someone speaks — is strongly associated with increased learning. When teachers give their students more time to think about their questions, students learn more. It's true at home, too.

- ✔ **Share a strategy.** After your child explains her thinking, talk about your own. Don't tell her how she needs to do something; just tell her in the spirit of sharing your own ideas. It's like being at the dinner table. When you want your child to share something that happened during the day, you model it by sharing your own stories from the day. It's the same with thinking. If you want your child to engage with English homework, you can model that behaviour by talking about how *you* think about the problems or the text you've just read.

Becoming unstuck: What to do

A few of the more stressful parenting moments include when time is tight and when your child is struggling with a homework assignment. Instead of cursing the heavens, Shakespeare and the originators of homework, you need a strategy. Here is a good one, in three parts:

- ✔ **Listen:** Ask your child to tell you what she is supposed to do. If something needs to be done a particular way, listen to what it is. Ask what she knows and doesn't know and then listen to the response. Don't try to tell her what to do or show her the way that you remember from school. Just listen.

- ✔ **Help:** After you have listened, decide how you can help. Sometimes you may have to show your child the way you learned to do something. Sometimes you may have to look something up online together. Sometimes you may have to phone a friend — your child's friend who may have an idea about what to do or your friend who may have some expertise. Don't assume that the way you learned is the best way (nor that it is the worst). An alternate way of working through something may help a child understand the meaning of what she's reading.

- ✔ **Let it go:** You and your child shouldn't be expected to spend your evenings engaged in tears and combat in the name of grammar facts. As a parent, model good study habits by establishing that some time will be spent doing what is assigned. You also should model good mental health habits by setting limits on that time. When your child is no longer making productive progress, let this homework go. You can write a note to the teacher explaining the decision that you have made and get on with the rest of your evening.

If getting stuck is a rare or occasional thing, letting it go is a good strategy to practice. If your child is regularly getting stuck on her homework and you find yourself letting it go on a regular basis, you probably need to have a conference with your child's teacher so that you each understand the demands being placed on your child. Frequent homework struggles can be a sign that your child needs something different from what she's getting at school. In such a case, you and your child's teacher should figure out how to work together to get her what she needs.

Chapter 2

Vivid Verbs

. . . .

In This Chapter

▶ Identifying action, linking and compound verbs

▶ Considering subjects

▶ Understanding subject–verb agreement

▶ Working with verbals

. . . .

*E*very sentence needs a *verb*. This group of words refers to actions, conditions or states of being to tell you what's happening in the sentence. And the verb connects with another group of words (called the *subject*) to tell you who performs the action of the verb.

Verbs are at the core of a sentence, and you should start with the verb when you want to do anything to your sentence — including correct it. So, in this chapter we look at different types of verbs, how to find them and how they fit together with subjects.

Verifying Verbs

Verbs come in various shapes and sizes — action and linking, auxiliary and main, regular and irregular, singular and plural. They can be present, past and future. The *tense* of a verb tells you when the action is happening. Making sure that you have the right verb in the right place is the key to understanding sentences. So in this section, we're going to reacquaint you with the different types of verbs, show how they often hang out together in groups, and give you the lowdown on how to locate the verb in a sentence.

Happening with action verbs

Action verbs are the real 'doing words'. Something happens in a sentence with an action verb:

> Chris *buys* and then *devours* three pasties as a snack. (*Buys* and *devours* are action verbs.)

> Ed *had answered* the question even before it *was asked*. (*Had answered* and *was asked* are action verbs.)

Don't let the name *action* fool you. Some action verbs aren't particularly energetic: *think, sit, stay, have, sleep, dream* and so on. Besides describing the perfect day off, these words are also action verbs.

Being with linking verbs

Not all verbs are as busy as action verbs. *Linking verbs* are also called *being verbs* because they express states of being — *what is, will be* or *was*. (Not surprisingly, the verb used to express the state of being is often the verb *to be*.) You can think of a linking verb as an equals sign in the middle of your sentence. In the same way that an equals sign tells you that the parts on either side of it are the same value, the word *is* links two ideas and says that those ideas are the same. For example:

> Yasmin *is* a smart young woman. (Yasmin = a smart young woman; *is* = linking verb.)

> Bobo *will be* angry if you take away her hair straightener. (Bobo = angry; *will be* is a linking verb.)

> Midge *was* the last surfer to leave the water. (Midge = last surfer; *was* is a linking verb.)

Not all linking verbs are forms of the verb *to be*. Other verbs work in the same way — check out these examples:

> With his twinkling eyes and shy smile, Damian *seems* harmless. (Damian = harmless; *seems* is a linking verb.)

> Lucinda's parents *remained* confident. (Lucinda's parents = confident; *remained* is a linking verb.)

Seems and *remained* are expressing states of being, so they're linking verbs too. Any verb that works as an equals sign in the sentence is a linking verb.

Sensory verbs — verbs that express information you receive through the senses of sight, hearing, smell, taste and touch — may also be linking verbs:

> Even after a bath to remove all the jam, Teddy still *feels* sticky. (Teddy = sticky; *feels* is a linking verb.)

> Uri's violin solo *sounds* horrible, like an animal in pain. (Uri's violin solo = horrible; *sounds* is a linking verb.)

Some verbs can act as both linking and action verbs — obviously not at the same time. Verbs, especially those that refer to the five senses, may be linking verbs, but only if they are equating two ideas. In the sentence about Teddy, *feels* is a linking verb. Here's a different sentence with the same verb:

> Yasmin *feels* the silk of Stella's new dress.

In this sentence, *feels* is not a linking verb because you're not saying:

> Yasmin = silk

Instead, you're saying that Yasmin is admiring Stella's dress and can't help touching the material.

Which sentence has a linking verb?

A. Fang smells every tree we pass on our daily walk.

B. Fang smells mouldy after a swim.

Answer: Sentence B has the linking verb. In sentence B, Fang = mouldy. In sentence A, Fang is *doing* something — smelling every tree — not *being*. (Well, he's probably being really annoying, but that information isn't in the sentence.)

Here's a list of the most common linking verbs:

- Forms of *to be*: am, are, is, was, were, will be, shall be, has been, have been, had been, could be, should be, would be, might have been, could have been, should have been, shall have been, will have been, must have been, must be

- Sensory verbs: look, sound, taste, smell, feel

- Words that express shades of meaning in reference to a state of being: appear, grow, remain, seem, stay, turn

Helping out in verb groups

You've probably noticed that some of the verbs identified throughout this chapter (such as *devours* and *remain*) are single words and others (such as *will answer* and *has made*) are made up of more than one word. The extra words are called *helping verbs* or *auxiliary verbs*. They help the main verb express meaning, usually changing the time, or *tense*, of the action. (For more on tense, see Chapter 3.) These groups of verbs can be called *compound verbs*, but we're going to refer to them by the very user-friendly and logical name *verb groups*.

Here is a sentence with verb groups:

> He *had been singing* karaoke all evening, and *should have stopped* after the first song. (In *had been singing*, *singing* is the main verb; *had* and *been* are auxiliary verbs. In the verb group *should have stopped*, *stopped* is the main verb.)

Without auxiliary verbs, we would still understand the general idea of the sentence from the main verb. *He singing karaoke all evening* conveys the sense of action and meaning, but it's not a grammatically correct sentence.

Sometimes, your grammar checker may warn that your sentence contains a 'split verb phrase'. Here's what it's trying to tell you. The parts of the verb group in the sentence have been separated by other words, as in these examples:

> Jules *was* totally *confused* by her reply. (*Was* = auxiliary; *confused* = main verb.)

> Jules *will* also *have* completely *missed* the clues. (*Will* = auxiliary; *have* = auxiliary; *missed* = main verb.)

Rest assured that this is not a mistake. Split verb phrases are a regular feature of our language landscape. The reason you should look again at your sentence and consider revising it is that in formal English the parts of the verb group should be kept together. So the sample sentences become:

> Jules *was confused* totally by her reply.

> Jules also *will have missed* the clues completely.

These formal sentences don't seem to emphasise the same points though, do they? And the meaning of the split verb versions is perfectly clear. So, consider whether or not to revise the sentence according to your audience and why you split the verb in the first place.

Finding the whole verb

When you try to crack a sentence, you should always start by identifying the verb. To find the verb, read the sentence and ask two questions:

- ✔ What's happening?
- ✔ What is? (*or* What word is acting as a giant equals sign?)

If you get an answer to the first question, you have an action verb. If you get an answer to the second question, you have a linking verb. Check the following sentence:

> Archie flew around the room and then swooped into his cage for a birdseed snack.

If you ask 'What's happening?' your answer is *flew* (*Archie ... flew*) and *swooped* (*Archie ... swooped*). *Flew* and *swooped* are action verbs.

If you ask 'What is?' you get no answer because no linking verb is in the sentence.

Try another:

> Bill's new tattoo will be larger than his previous nine tattoos.

What's happening? Nothing. You have no action verb. What is? Look for the equals sign:

> Bill's new tattoo = larger

The words that stand for the equals sign are *will be*. So *will be* is a linking verb.

Have a go at finding the verbs in the following sentences. Then identify the verbs as action or linking.

- **A.** Bobo loved the cat, even though the cat had scratched her furniture to ribbons.
- **B.** After days of inactivity, Midge is taking a skiing holiday.
- **C.** The twisted frown on Ellie's face seemed strange, but she was listening to Uri's violin solo on her headphones.

Answers: A. *loved* and *had scratched* are both action verbs. B. *is taking* is an action verb. C. *seemed* is a linking verb and *was listening* is an action verb.

Simplifying Subjects

All complete sentences contain verbs — words that express action or state of being. So, someone or something must also be present in the sentence doing the action or being of that verb. The *who* or *what* you're talking about in relation to the action or state of being expressed by the verb is the *subject*. In this section, we're going to show you how to locate the subject, even if it's hiding out somewhere sneaky.

Locating the subject

The first question to ask about a sentence is *What's the verb?* To find the verb, you need to ask *What's happening?* or *What is?* After you uncover the verb, ask *who* or *what* is doing it. The answer to that question is the subject!

Try one:

> Jonah straightens his hair every day.

1. **Ask yourself the question:** What's happening?

   Answer: *Straightens. Straightens* is the verb.

2. **Ask yourself:** Who or what *straightens*?

   Answer: *Jonah* straightens. *Jonah* is the subject.

A subject is always a *noun* (person, place, thing or idea) or a noun equivalent. A 'someone' is always a person and a 'something' is a thing, place or idea. When the subject is a noun equivalent, it is a *pronoun* (a word such as *she*, *they* or *it* that substitutes for a noun) or a noun group (a group of words doing the work of a noun).

Baring the complete subject

In squillions of sentences, the subject contains more than just one word. For example:

> That huge slice of gooey chocolate mud cake looks delicious.

To identify the subject in this sentence, we first locate the verb (*looks*) and then ask the subject question (*Who* or *what* looks?). Now, the answer to the subject question for this sentence is a bit tricky. Is it *That huge slice of gooey chocolate mud cake* or is it simply *cake*? Both answers are actually correct.

That huge slice of gooey chocolate mud cake is known as the *complete subject*. The complete subject contains all the words that give information about the person or thing performing the verb. The complete subject is also a *noun group*, a group of words doing the same job as a single-word noun in a sentence.

The single-word subject (in this case *cake*) is known as the *simple subject* or the *bare subject*. It's the complete subject after having been stripped naked. Bare of any and all extra information and decoration, the subject is always simply a noun or a pronoun (which stand in for nouns).

Uncovering a hidden subject

Although the subject usually comes before the verb, not every sentence follows that order. Sometimes (especially if you're having a conversation with Yoda from *Star Wars*) a subject hides at the end of the sentence or in some other weird place. Consider this:

> At the water's edge stood several confused Jedi knights.

The verb in this sentence is *stood* but it's not the water's edge doing the standing, it's the Jedi knights. Here, the subject follows the verb. Tricky, huh?

If you ask yourself who or what is performing the verb, and answer that question according to the meaning of the sentence — not according to the word order — you'll be fine. The key is to put the subject questions (who? what?) in front of the verb. Then think about what the sentence is actually saying. And voila! Your subject will appear.

Commanding an understood subject

Consider the following:

> Be quiet.

> Give me that.

What do these sentences have in common? Yes, they're all bossy comments you've heard all your life. More importantly, they're all commands. The verbs give orders: *be, give*. So where's the subject in these sentences?

Here's what happens:

1. **Ask yourself:** What's happening? What is?

   Answer: *Be, give.*

2. **Ask yourself:** Who *be, give?*

   Answer: Ummmm . . .

The second question appears to have no answer, but you do know who's supposed to be doing these things (or who's not doing them): *You.* They mean *You* be quiet. *You* give me that. Grammarians say that the subject is *understood.* The subject is *you,* even though *you* isn't in the sentence and even though *you* may choose not to hear any of the commands.

Making Subjects and Verbs Agree

Subjects and verbs must form pairs. In grammar this process is called *agreement.* The verb must match up with, or *agree,* with the subject. Your ear for proper language likely allows you to create these subject–verb pairs without much thought. Helping you is the fact that, in most cases, you use exactly the same form of the verb for both singular and plural verbs. In this section, we focus on how to be a good matchmaker of subject–verb pairs.

To find the subject–verb pair, first find the verb. Ask yourself the verb question: *What's happening?* or *What is?* The answer is the verb. Then ask the subject question: *Who* or *what is performing the verb?* The answer is the subject.

Separating singles from plurals

English verbs are adjusted a little to match their subject — the person or thing performing the verb. So we say *John leaps* when just one John is doing the leaping (John is *singular*). But we say *the dancers leap* when more than one person is leaping (*dancers* is *plural*). Notice how, in these sample sentences, singular subjects (just one) are matched with singular verbs, and plural subjects (more than one) are matched with plural verbs:

Gerard the garden gnome loves the fairy. (*Gerard* = singular subject, *loves* = singular verb)

His kookaburra friends laugh at him. (*friends* = plural subject, *laugh* = plural verb)

Never try to match a singular subject with a plural verb or vice versa. The result is a disastrous mismatch.

The pronoun *you* can refer to one person (singular) or to a group (plural). This can cause confusion, which is why people sometimes add '... I don't mean "you" personally ...' to make it clear that they didn't mean any insult specifically to the person they were speaking to — they were just generally insulting the whole family or all their school friends!

Adjusting verbs to match subjects

In English, the verb shows the time the action or 'being' took place — past, present or future — and whether that action is finished or on-going. We call this *verb tense* and grammar has lots of special labels to identify all the possible variations. We're not going to bore you with all the details. Quite honestly, you don't even need to know the labels to be able to make subjects and verbs agree, but you'll find them with the examples just in case seeing them helps you to learn (or remember) better grammar.

Remaining regular

Many verbs fit into the category known as *regular verbs*. They don't need much adjusting to match up with subjects. Here are some examples, all with the regular verb *to snore*, of tenses that use the same form for both singular and plural subjects:

Cassie *snored* constantly, but her cousins *snored* only on long weekends. (The *simple past tense* verb *snored* matches both the singular subject Cassie and the plural subject *cousins*.)

Peter *will snore* if he eats cheese before bed, but his *budgies will snore* whenever they fall asleep. (The *simple future* tense verb *will snore* matches both the singular subject *Peter* and the plural subject *budgies*.)

Peter *had snored* long before his tonsils were removed, but on sleepovers all his school friends *had snored* too. (The *past perfect* verb *had snored* matches both the singular subject *Peter* and the plural subject *school friends*.)

By the time the movie is over, Peter *will have snored* for at least ten minutes, and his budgies *will have snored* for even longer. (The *future perfect* verb *will have snored* matches both the singular subject *Peter* and the plural subject *budgies*.)

Nearly all regular verbs are the same for both singular and plural. The singular verb ends in *s* and the plural form doesn't. Here are some examples of regular present tense verbs:

Singular	Plural
the dog bites	the dogs bite
Lucinda rides	they ride
he screams	the boys scream

Changing irregularly

Unfortunately, communication would be severely limited if you stuck to just the unchanging tenses. Even though irregular verbs (the ones that don't follow a regular pattern) are the minority, they are a pretty important and often powerful little group — *I bring, he (bringed??) brought; he gives, they (gived??) gave.* The most used verb in the English language is *to be*, and it's the most irregular of all. So Table 2-1 sets it out for you. (Chapter 3 covers verb tenses in more detail.)

Verbs that end in *-ing* — *continuous tenses* — can cause problems. These tenses rely on the verb *to be*. Always take care to match the subject to the correct form of the verb *to be*. Examples are: *I am trying, we were trying, they had been trying, you will be trying.*

Another group of verbs (that possibly have fairly fat heads because they're called *perfect tenses*) contain forms of the irregular verb *to have*. Be careful to use the correct form of this irregular verb too. Examples are: I *have bitten,* you *have bitten,* Spike *has bitten, we have bitten,* the wombats *have bitten.*

Table 2-1	Singular and Plural Forms of the Verb 'To Be'	
Tense	**Singular**	**Plural**
Present	I am	we are
	you are	you are
	he, she, it is	they are
Past	I was	we were
	you were	you were
	he, she, it was	they were

Tense	Singular	Plural
Future	I will be	we will be
	you will be	you will be
	he, she, it will be	they will be
Present perfect	I have been	we have been
	you have been	you have been
	he, she, it has been	they have been
Past perfect	I had been	we had been
	you had been	you had been
	he, she, it had been	they had been
Future perfect	I will have been	we will have been
	you will have been	you will have been
	he, she, it will have been	they will have been

Matching two subjects

Just as a sentence can have one subject matched with more than one verb, so too a sentence can have more than one subject matched with just one verb. Two (or more) subjects joined by *and* usually take a plural verb, even if each of the subjects is singular. (Think of maths: 1 + 1 = 2. One subject + one subject = plural subject.) Here's how it works:

> Gerard and the fairy belong together. (*Gerard* + *fairy* = plural subject, *belong* = plural verb)

> Ando and Johnno plan to gnome-nap Gerard. (*Ando* + *Johnno* = plural subject, *plan* = plural verb)

Time is money and they're both singular

Time and money are the same, at least in grammar. Treat them as singular whenever you refer to them as a lump. So:

Fifty minutes *is* not enough for a television documentary about potato chips.

A thousand dollars *was* a powerful temptation to Lucinda, and she decided to appear wearing a paper bag.

But money is plural when you talk about it as a physical thing — separate notes or coins. For example:

Two five-dollar notes *are* taped inside Damian's cricket jacket because he thinks that they bring him luck.

One hundred francs *were* wrapped carefully, one by one and with great ceremony, and added to Cedric's coin collection.

Looking like Verbs: Verbals

All sorts of words like to stay fit by functioning as several different parts of speech, depending on how they are used. *Verbals* may look like verbs, or even be part of a verb group, but on their own, they don't perform any verb jobs in a sentence. In this section, we look at the three key verb-impersonators.

The most important thing to know about verbals is this: When you ask the question to find the verb, don't choose a verbal as your answer. If you do, you'll miss the real verb or verbs in the sentence.

Participating with participles

Participles are actually parts of verbs (hence the amazingly original name) that are not directly connected to the subject of the verb. So, when participles appear without the support of auxiliary or helping verbs, they act as adjectives (modifying nouns and noun equivalents). Here's how to recognise one:

- ✔ Participles look like verbs and can indicate present or past. *Present participles* end with *-ing*: *coping, blushing, posing*. Some *past participles* end with *-ed* (those from regular verbs such as *coped, blushed, posed*). Some end with other letters (those from *irregular verbs* such as *driven, gone, broken*).

- ✔ They have auxiliary verbs. For example: *had been* trying, *is* taken, *was* stuck, *will be* completed.

Naming gerunds

Occasionally, those -*ing* participles from the preceding section like to function as nouns. When they do this, they're called *gerunds*. Sounds more like a little furry creature than a tricky two-timing verb form, doesn't it? All gerunds end in -*ing* — *swimming, dripping, fishing, dancing, singing* and so on.

Here are a few examples, with the gerund and all the words associated with it (the *gerund phrase*) italicised:

> *Swimming* is not foremost in Midge's mind; he prefers *surfing*. (*swimming* = subject of the verb *is*; *surfing* = subject of the verb *prefers*)

> Bobo, a generous person in every other way, hates *sharing her food*. (*sharing her food* = object of the verb *hates*)

> The importance of *remaining calm* can't be overemphasised. (*remaining calm* = object of the preposition *of*)

One gerund-related and very old-school rule is still respected by some modern grammar checkers, but confuses many modern writers. It has to do with the way we use pronouns with gerunds. Here's an example:

> WRONG: I hope you don't mind me asking.

> RIGHT: I hope you don't mind my asking.

As for many grammar rules, this distinction is all but extinct in casual communication. It should still be applied, however, in formal written documents. Here's how it works.

In the preceding sample sentence, the -*ing* word is a gerund. It is doing the work of a noun. Let's substitute another noun in its place to prove it:

> I hope you don't mind my questions.

See? They mean exactly the same thing. The sentence doesn't ask whether you're disturbed by *me*. It asks whether you're disturbed by *the asking*. And that's the trick to trying to decide how to revise the sentence. Try replacing the pronoun in front of a gerund with the word *the*. If it sounds comfortable, your -*ing* word is doing the work of a noun; it's a gerund. The only pronouns you can legally use in front of a gerund are *my, your, his, her, their* or *our*.

Defining infinitives

The *infinitive* is the *base form of a verb* (the *to* form) but like a singer without a band, it can't do the job of a verb unless it's supported by auxiliary or helping verbs in a verb group. Infinitives look like verbs, with the word *to* tacked on in front — *to dance, to dream, to be, to dally* and so on.

The following examples of infinitives in their natural habitat, the sentence, may help you to identify them. The infinitive and the words associated with it (called the *infinitive phrase*) are in italics:

> Lucinda *likes to spend.* (*to spend* = the object of the verb *likes*)
>
> *To sing on* The X Factor is Willem's lifelong dream. (*to sing on* The X Factor = the subject of the verb *is*)
>
> Macca's goal is *to be unemployed forever.* (*to be unemployed forever* = the subject complement of the verb *is*)

It used to be considered a grammar crime to split the infinitive. This 'rule' is a hangover from Latin-loving grammarians who insisted that because in Latin a to-infinitive was a single word (which, of course, couldn't be split), it must still never be split. The grammar checker on your computer may let you break the old rule a little bit and tell you that no more than one word should stand between the *to* and the verb part of a *to*-infinitive. However, the meaning of your sentence may depend on whether or not the 'rule' is applied.

Consider these examples:

> Gina expects *to* more than *double* her wealth monthly. (split)
>
> Gina expects more than *to double* her wealth monthly. (not split)

The first sentence means 'Gina looks forward to her bank balance increasing by at least the power of two every month' — *more than* is modifying *double*. The second sentence is saying 'Gina greedily anticipates even more than the monthly doubling of her bank balance' — *more than* is modifying *expects*. Not the same meaning at all. Sorry computer, epic fail!

See if you can work out which of the following three sentences would be best:

A. Lucinda vowed to study really if she ever got the chance to take her exams again.

B. Lucinda vowed really to study if she ever got the chance to take her exams again.

C. Lucinda vowed to really study if she ever got the chance to take her exams again.

Answers: Sentence C has a split, but it's the best of the three. Sentence A isn't split but doesn't work because it makes *really* sound like the subject Lucinda's studying. Sentence B isn't split either, but it sounds as if she *vowed really*.

So splitting the infinitive is perfectly acceptable, especially if it enhances your meaning or makes the sentence sound comfortable and natural.

Are you affected or effected?

Has the study of grammar *affected* or *effected* your brain? These two words are an annoyance, but help is at hand. In most cases, *affect* is a verb meaning to influence and *effect* is a noun meaning result. Hence:

> Sunlight *affects* Drac's appetite; he never eats during the day.

> Sasha thinks her herbal tea will *affect* Drac's lack of appetite, but I think the *effect* may surprise her.

To help you remember the difference, use the mnemonic RAVEN. It stands for:

Remember

Affect

Verb

Effect

Noun

Of course, just to complicate matters, in specific circumstances *affect* can also be a noun. It means *the way you relate to and show emotions*, but you can pretty much forget about it unless you're studying psychology. And *effect* can be a verb. It means *to bring about or accomplish*.

> The company accountants fear there could be problems when they effect the changeover to the new pay system.

This use is so old-fashioned that your computer is likely to think it's a mistake. It's not wrong, but it does sound pompous — simpler words are better choices.

Chapter 3

Timing is Everything: Understanding Verb Tense

*Y*ou can tell the time in lots of ways: look at a clock, calculate the height of the sun, check your phone . . . or check the verb. The verb shows the action or state of being in the sentence. In English, the verb also shows the time the action or 'being' took place. (For more information on finding the verb in a sentence, refer to Chapter 2.)

Three of the six English tenses (*present*, *past* and *future*) are called *simple* — not 'simple' as in easy, 'simple' as in a pretty technical grammatical version of the word! In this chapter, we explain the simple tenses in some detail, such as the difference between *I go* and *I am going*. We also cover active and passive voice and how this works in with verb choice.

Simplifying Matters: The Simple Tenses

The three simple tenses are present, past and future. Each of the simple tenses (just to make things even more fun) has two forms. One is the unadorned, no-frills, plain tense. This form doesn't have a separate name; it's just called present, past or future. It shows actions or states of being at a point in time, but it doesn't always pin down a specific moment. The other form is called continuous. The continuous form shows an action or a state of being in progress.

Simple present tense

The present tense tells you what's going on at the present time. It describes an action or state of being that's occurring right now, or that's generally true, or that happens all the time, like a habit, but may not be taking place at this very second.

English verbs are adjusted a little to match their subject — the person or thing performing the verb. But most verbs don't change much in the present tense. The verb *to work*, for example, goes something like this: I *work*, you *work*, he (or she or it) *works*, we *work*, you (plural) *work*, they *make a fortune* . . . er, they *work*.

As you can see, a version with an extra *s* on the end (*works*) occurs once, but mostly it's just work! work! work! Take a look at these sentences in the no-frills present tense:

What does Irma's cat *want*? It just *sits* there and *stares* at me. (*Want, sits* and *stares* are all in the present tense. *Want* is happening now. *Sits* and *stares* are generally true or habitual, but the cat may be nowhere about at this moment.)

Ed *plans* nothing for New Year's Eve because he never *has* a date. (*Plans* and *has* are in the present tense. Both verbs express actions that are always true — or never true in Ed's case — but today is not necessarily New Year's Eve.)

The *-ing* form of the verb is traditionally called the *present participle* (more on this in the next section). Here are three sentences in the present continuous form:

Fang and Bluey *are chasing* Fluffy. (*Are chasing* is in the present continuous form.)

'I *am doing* my work,' insists Lucinda, but her classmates suspect that she *is emailing* a friend instead. (*Am doing* and *is emailing* are in the present continuous form.)

Progress on and you'll be rewarded with more details about using these forms presently, in the following sections.

Simple past tense

The past tense expresses what happened before the present time. As with present tense (refer to preceding section), this simple tense also has two forms — *plain past* and *past continuous*. The past tense is often formed by adding *-ed* to the basic form of the verb (*walk* becomes *walked*). And that's it. There aren't even two forms of the verb in the past tense, just the one (*I walked*, *she walked*). The bad news is that lots of verbs have a past tense that doesn't end with *-ed*. They're called *irregular* verbs, and we cover them back in Chapter 2.

Here are some sentences in the *plain past* tense:

> When the elastic in Ms Stakes's pants *snapped*, we all *felt* ill. (*Snapped* is regular past tense and *felt* is irregular past tense.)

> Sandy *got* a job as a part-time lifeguard at the local swimming pool and *started* last Saturday. (*Got* is irregular past tense and *started* is regular past tense.)

The *past continuous* form may pinpoint action or state of being at a specific time or occurring in the past on a regular basis. It consists of the past tense of the verb *to be* (*I was*, *you were* and so on) as the auxiliary, plus the *-ing* form of the main verb:

> While Bill *was sleeping*, Fang *was* completely *destroying* the garden. (*Was sleeping* and *was destroying* are in the continuous form of the past tense.)

> Erin's workmates *were planning* their revenge. (*Were planning* is in the continuous form of the past tense.)

The *-ing* form of the verb is often called the *present participle*. The examples in the preceding section use it to form the *present continuous* tense but, in this section, the examples use it to form the *past continuous*. (And we're about to use it to form the *future* continuous.) So what's 'present' about it? Nothing really. (It would make more sense to call it a *continuous* participle.) Your English is teacher is likely aware of this. Some teachers just say that it's 'traditionally' called the present participle and then turn away feigning disinterest; others call it the *-ing form* (which may be just a little bit ugly and awkward but at least it doesn't claim to be doing something that it isn't). So, if you know perfectly well what an *-ing* does but can't remember the term *present participle*, don't worry.

You can't do much wrong with the past tense, except maybe with the irregular ones, but a very common mistake is to mix past and present tenses in the same story, which can prompt the computer message 'Incorrect verb tenses'. Here's an example:

> So I go to the restaurant looking for Lucinda because I want to fill her in about Ed's date with Yasmin. I walk in and who's right there? Yasmin! So I went up to her but, before I got to her table, Damian appeared out of nowhere and sat down opposite her.

The speaker started in the present tense — no problem. Even though an event is clearly over, the present tense is okay if you want to make a story sound more dramatic. But the last sentence switches gears — suddenly we're in the past tense. Problem. Don't change tenses in the middle of a story, not even if you're gossiping.

Simple future tense

The *future tense* talks about what hasn't happened yet. This simple tense is the only one that always needs helping verbs to express meaning, even for the plain no-frills version. (That's why the experts who claim only two tenses exist say this isn't a tense at all.) Future tenses also come in two forms: the *future* and the *future continuous*.

For the plain form of the future, put *will* (or, for casual language, *'ll* — which is short for *will*) in front of the basic form of the verb. Look at these sentences:

> Damian's sister *will lose* patience with him soon. (*Will lose* is in the future tense.)

> I'*ll do* it myself. (*'ll do* is in the future tense.)

For the *future continuous*, we put *will be* (or *'ll be*) in front of the present participle (the *-ing* form of the verb) like this:

> While she waits for her test results, Yasmin *will be considering* her options for the future. (*Will be considering* is in the continuous form of the future tense.)

> I'*ll be eating* out tonight. (*'ll be eating* is in the continuous form of the future tense.)

Find the verbs in the following sentences and sort them into simple present, past and future tenses:

A. When the rain starts, the fun stops and everyone runs for cover.

B. Will you pay?

C. Fang ate Bill's dinner and buried Jane's slippers in the garden.

Answers: In sentence A, *starts*, *stops* and *runs* are present tense verbs. In sentence B, *will pay* is in the future tense. In sentence C, *ate* and *buried* are in the past tense.

Now find the verbs in the following and sort them into present continuous, past continuous and future continuous forms:

A. Possums in football boots were dancing on our roof last night.

B. They are spending way too much on this renovation.

C. They will be flying to Fiji for their honeymoon.

Answers: In sentence A, *were dancing* is a past continuous verb. In sentence B, *are spending* is in the present continuous form. In C, *will be flying* is in the future continuous form.

Using the Tenses Correctly

What's the difference between each pair of simple tense forms? Not a lot. People often interchange these forms without creating any problems. But shades of difference in meaning do exist.

Continuous tense

The three simple tenses are present, past and future. Each of the simple tenses (just to make things even *more* fun) has two forms. One is the unadorned, no-frills, plain tense. This form doesn't have a separate name; it's just called *present, past* or *future*. It shows actions or states of being at a point in time, but it doesn't always pin down a specific moment. The other form is called *continuous*. The continuous form shows an action or a state of being *in progress*.

Past continuous

The difference between the plain past tense and the past continuous tense is pretty much the same as for the present tense. The single-word form often shows what happened in the past more generally. The continuous form may refer to what happened or existed at a specific time or occurred in the past on a regular basis.

Lucinda *went* to the shops and *bought* gifts for all her friends.

This sentence means that at some point in the past Lucinda splurged on presents for her friends (*went* and *bought* are in past tense).

While Lucinda *was shopping*, her friends *were planning* the food for her surprise party.

This sentence means that Lucinda has chosen her friends well because, at the exact moment she was spending her pocket money on them, her friends were planning something nice for her (*was shopping* and *were planning* are in the continuous form of the past tense).

> Damian *was losing* so much money on bets with his brother that his sister *was feeling* sorry for him.

This sentence refers to one of Damian's bad habits, his gambling, and the effect it was having on his sister (*was losing* and *was feeling* are in the continuous form of the past tense). The betting and the feeling desperate were repeated, over and over again (until, finally, Damian's sister made him see the error of his ways).

Present continuous

The single-word form of the present tense may be used for things that are generally true at the present time but not necessarily happening right now. For example:

> Bill *attends* wrestling matches every Saturday.

Attends is in present tense so, if you call Bill on Saturday, you'll get an annoying message on his answering machine because he's at the wrestling. You may also get that message on a Friday (or any other day) and it will still be correct, even though on Fridays Bill stays home to watch football on television and doesn't answer his phone. Now read this sentence:

> Bill *is playing* hide-and-seek with his dog Spot.

This sentence means that right now, as you read this sentence (*is playing* is in the continuous form of the present tense), Bill is running around looking for Spot.

Future continuous

You won't find much difference between the future and future continuous, except that the continuous can give you more of a sense of being in the middle of things. Check this example:

> Rashid *will play* Hamlet in the local amateur production.

Here, *will play* is in the future tense, so the sentence may be an official announcement that Rashid has the part, even if rehearsals haven't started yet and the performances are still a few months away. Now read this sentence:

Rashid *will be playing* Hamlet in the local amateur production.

Here, *will be playing* is in the continuous form of the future tense, suggesting that we're much nearer to the event (you wouldn't be surprised if this sentence had *tomorrow* on the end of it).

Finding the Right Voice: Active and Passive

Verbs can have two voices — and we're not talking about piercing, or whiny, or nasal or baritone, or husky type voices. With verbs, *voice* means the way the verb behaves with respect to its subject. Verbs are in either *active* or *passive voice*. Take a look at these two examples:

'The window *was broken* yesterday,' reported Richard, carefully tucking his cricket bat under the couch.

'I *broke* the window yesterday,' reported Richard, hoping that his parents wouldn't be too angry.

How do the two sentences differ? Well, in one case Richard is hoping he won't be blamed and in the other he's confessing. Grammatically, Richard's statement in the first version focuses on the receiver of the verb's action, the *window*, which received the action of the verb *was broken*. The verb is *passive* (in *passive voice*) because the subject of the sentence isn't the person or thing doing the action. Instead, the subject is the person or thing receiving the action of the verb. In the second version the verb is in the *active voice* because the subject (*I*) performed the action (*broke*). When the subject is acting or being, the verb is *active*.

To find the subject of a sentence, locate the verb and ask *who* or *what ...?* (insert the verb). For more information on subjects and verbs refer to Chapter 2.

Here are some active and passive verbs:

Lucinda *is convinced* by Damian to get a tattoo. (passive — clueless Lucinda is receiving the convincing)

> Rashid *talks* Lucinda out of it. (active — conservative Rashid is doing the talking)
>
> Damian *is tattooed* by Bill. (passive — bad boy Damian is receiving the tattooing)

Some people loathe the passive voice. They insist that the active voice is direct, honest and more powerful, and that the passive is evasive and takes more words. In fact, sometimes the passive is not just acceptable: it's preferable. Everyone accepts that if you don't know the facts, the passive comes in handy:

> Little progress *has been made* in the investigation of the burglary at Ms Stakes's, the local teacher whose garden gnome went missing a year ago today. (This example, using passive voice, is 26 words. You'll notice that in passive voice, the verbs have auxiliaries. Parts of the verb *to be* are the auxiliary verbs in the passive voice — *has been, was*.)

The passive version doesn't say who has made little progress, but you can guess the subject is probably police. It has no specific information about the burglar because he (or she) hasn't been identified yet; the sentence contains all the information available.

People who are against passive voice claim that using passive voice misleads people because it leaves out the performer of the verb (in this case, the police and the burglar). But this example isn't misleading at all. By not mentioning the police, the passive version emphasises the lack of progress, which is the problem. And, by not mentioning the burglar, it emphasises the crime. Opponents of passive voice also say that it's more wordy than the forthright active voice. Well, here's the active-voice version:

> Police *have made* little progress in their investigation of the burglary at Ms Stakes's residence. An unknown person *removed* the local teacher's garden gnome a year ago today. (This active version has 28 words — okay, 26 if you say *someone* instead of *an unknown person*.)

Both versions are about the same length, and the active voice version has neither the focus nor the impact of the passive version. Sometimes, choosing passive voice allows you to focus on what's most important.

But the strongest argument for using active voice is that the passive is evasive — it avoids giving information. Look at these sentences:

> It *has been recommended* that the servicing of the heating system be postponed until next year. (Passive: 16 words)
>
> Ron *recommended* that the servicing of the heating system be postponed until next year. (Active: 14 words)

In the first (passive) sentence, no-one is taking responsibility. If the central heating breaks down, nobody knows who to blame. In the second (active) sentence, the building's residents know exactly who to blame if they're freezing. It's all Ron's fault. Sometimes it's handy to be able to hide behind a passive sentence. Ask Ron!

Here are examples of when to choose the passive voice:

✔ If it's not clear who performed the action:

The glass eye was found on the beach.

✔ If it's not necessary to know who or what performed the action:

Sugar was added to the mixture.

✔ To emphasise the someone or something that suffered the action:

The politician was forced to eat his own words.

✔ To create a sense of distance and avoid taking blame for the action:

Your request for a refund has been denied.

If you're not trying to do any of the preceding, choose active voice. Active voice takes your reader in a straight line from one point to the other. Passive voice is less direct.

So what should you do if your grammar checker alerts you to the presence of passive voice and advises that you consider revising the sentence? Well, the obvious first port of call is to check your sentence against the preceding list of instances when passive voice is preferable. Then, if your sentence doesn't fit into any of those categories, here's an illustration of how to convert it to active voice:

The interview was conducted by Rupert himself.

Step one in the revision is to locate the verb group and remove the helping or auxiliary verb/s (we put a line through the word(s) to remove):

~~was~~ conducted

Step two is to locate the performer of the verb's action (the performer will be a noun or noun equivalent — but remember that sometimes in passive voice the performer of the verb's action isn't even mentioned, so you may have to add a subject). Then move the subject to the front of the main verb to create a subject–verb pair. You probably have to drop the preposition *by* completely:

~~by~~ *Rupert himself* ~~was~~ conducted

Step three is simply to add the rest of the sentence:

Rupert himself conducted the interview.

You have now converted the sentence to active voice, with the subject performing the verb's action.

You want to avoid shifting from active to passive voice in the same sentence. Consider the following:

My disgusting cat *stalks* drop-tail skinks and then their tails *are eaten* by her. (active + passive = wrong)

Drop-tail skinks *are stalked* by my disgusting cat and then their tails *are eaten* by her. (passive + passive = correct but not a very good sentence — or a very pleasant habit for a cat to have, just quietly — because this sentence does not need to be passive)

My disgusting cat *stalks* drop-tail skinks and then *eats* their tails. (active + active = correct and a better sentence)

Label the verbs in these sentences as active or passive.

A. The batter was made with egg yolks, but the whites were discarded.

B. Cassie slobbers when she eats eggs.

Answer: Sentence A is passive (*was made, were discarded*), and sentence B is active (*slobbers, eats*).

Try one more. Which is active and which is passive?

A. A nail has been hammered into his coffin.

B. Mildred is building a tank for her new pet piranhas.

Answer: Sentence A is passive (*has been hammered*), and sentence B is active (*is building*).

Chapter 4

Completing Sentences

· ·

In This Chapter

▷ Learning the elements of a complete sentence

▷ Exploring clauses

▷ Working with coordination and subordination

▷ Identifying sentence fragments

▷ Recognising prepositions and prepositional phrases

▷ Punctuating the end of sentences correctly

· ·

The most basic rule of English grammar is that all sentences must be complete.

But everyone breaks the rule. Often. Even people who write grammar books do it! *Often* isn't a complete sentence. It's a *sentence fragment*. But you understood it, didn't you? (That's an incomplete sentence.) Message received quite clearly. (Another sentence fragment.) In this chapter, you find out how to decide whether your sentence is grammatically complete, and how to identify clauses. You get to understand *sentence fragments*, and how to recognise prepositions and prepositional phrases. And then you discover everything you need to know about endmarks, the punctuation that separates one sentence from another.

Understanding Sentence Basics

A *sentence* is a group of words that contains at least one independent clause. It has a subject and a 'finite' verb, and makes complete sense by itself. (A finite verb is one that changes form to match its subject. It has tense, person and number. Participles without helping verbs are not finite. Refer to Chapters 2 and 3 for more.)

A *simple sentence* consists of one independent clause. A *compound sentence* has two or more independent clauses joined together. It contains two complete ideas of equal importance, and is usually joined with a coordinating conjunction. A *complex sentence* has one independent clause and one or more dependent clauses. A dependent clause begins with either a subordinating conjunction or a relative pronoun.

Let's look at some examples.

Simple Sentence	*Compound Sentence*	*Complex Sentence*
The wind howled.	The wind howled and the lightning flashed.	The wind that lashed the town came from the west.
Our dog hates storms.	Our dog hates storms but he loves fireworks.	Our dog barked because the thunder was ear-splitting.

You Complete Me: Subject and Verb Pairs

What makes a sentence complete? Well, a complete sentence has at least one subject–verb pair; they're a pair because they match up. That is, the subject and verb go together. The sentence must include one element expressing action or being (a verb), and one element that's performing the action or being (a subject). To make a correct pair, the verb must be written in a form that has a clear meaning when teamed with its subject. *They match* is a correct subject–verb pair with a clear meaning. But what if we said, *They to match*? You may be able to work out the meaning, but you can hear likely that the pair is not a proper team. Something is missing.

A subject plus verb pair that matches perfectly requires the type of verb that we lovers of good grammar like to call a *finite verb*. Finite verbs are adjusted to match up with a subject. (For more information on verbs, refer to Chapters 2 and 3.)

Some subject–verb pairs that match are:

> The team (subject) has lost (verb).
>
> Their supporters (subject) will swear (verb).
>
> Sweaty sport socks (subject) smell (verb).
>
> The captain of the team (subject) had goofed (verb).

Just for comparison, here's one mismatch:

Winners (subject) celebrating (verb).

The subject–verb pair doesn't match. The sentence doesn't make complete sense. Something is missing.

When you're checking a sentence for completeness, search for a matching subject–verb pair. If you can't find one, you don't have a complete sentence.

Complete sentences may also include more than one subject–verb pair:

Alice waited impatiently while Lucinda unlocked the door. (*Alice* = subject of the verb *waited*; *Lucinda* = the subject of the verb *unlocked*.)

Not only did Brad bowl but he also batted. (*Brad* = the subject of the verb *did bowl*; *he* = subject of the verb *batted*.)

Complete sentences may also match one subject with more than one verb, and vice versa:

Ellie appeared in three commercials but sang in only two. (*Ellie* = the subject of the verbs *appeared* and *sang*.)

Rusty and Fang fight endlessly over a bone. (*Rusty* and *Fang* = the subjects of the verb *fight*.)

Complete sentences that give commands may match an understood subject (*you*) with the verb:

Send an email to everyone who left details. (*You* = the understood subject of the verb *send*; *who* = the subject of the verb *left*.)

To find the subject–verb pair, first find the verb. Ask yourself the verb question: *What's happening?* or *What is?* The answer is the verb. Then ask the subject question: *Who* or *what is performing the verb?* The answer is the subject. (For a more complete explanation, refer to Chapter 3.)

The following sentence contains one correct subject–verb pair and one mismatch. Can you find the correct subject–verb pair?

The angry driver stuck in morning traffic swore never to take the freeway again.

Answer: The subject–verb pair is *driver swore*. The mismatch is *driver stuck*. The sentence isn't saying that the *driver stuck* something, so *driver stuck* isn't a match. In fact, the complete subject of the verb *swore* is *The angry driver stuck in morning traffic*.

Sentence trivia

The record for the longest sentence in English literature was in *Ulysses* by James Joyce, published in 1922. The sentence contained 4,391 words. However, Jonathan Coe's *The Rotters' Club*, published in 2001, contains a sentence with 13,955 words! One of the shortest sentences in the English language, containing a subject and a verb, is *I am*. However, the commands *Run!* or *Smile!* or *Stop!* are also sentences because they contain a verb and a subject that is 'understood' — *you* — even though it does not appear in the sentence. A sentence using every letter of the alphabet is known as a *pangram*. The best known is 'The quick brown fox jumps over the lazy dog'.

Expressing Complete Thoughts

It's not enough for a sentence to begin with a capital letter and end with a full stop. A complete sentence must express a complete thought, like this:

Despite Kylie's fragile appearance, she is a tough opponent.

Danni planned her attack.

She pounced.

Here are some incomplete thoughts, just for comparison:

The reason I should be the star.

Because I said so.

You may be thinking that both of the preceding incomplete thoughts could be part of a longer conversation. Yes, you're right. You can make these incomplete sentences grammatically complete by stating the ideas that the rest of the conversation gives you:

I explained the reason I should be the star, even though she was really only interested in trying on her glittery costume.

You have to clean up your desk because I said so.

So, now you know that every complete sentence must have at least one subject–verb pair and express a complete thought.

Clauses: Nothing to do with Santa

No matter what you put between two pieces of bread, you have a sandwich. That's the definition of sandwich: bread plus filling. Clauses have a simple definition too: subject plus *finite verb* (a verb that has been adjusted to match its noun). A *clause* is a complete unit of meaning within a sentence. Any subject–verb pair creates a clause. The reverse is also true: no subject or no verb — no clause. You can throw in some extras (descriptions, joining words, lettuce, tomato … whatever), but the basic subject–verb pair is the key. In this section, we look at how we use clauses to create complete sentences.

Identifying single and multiple clauses

Some sentences have one clause (in which case the whole sentence is the clause) and some sentences have more than one clause.

Here are a few examples of one-clause sentences:

> Shannon sings. (subject = *Shannon*, verb = *sings*)
>
> Has Mike found the woman of his dreams yet? (subject = *Mike*, verb = *has found*)
>
> Sandy sailed safely around the world single-handed. (subject = *Sandy*, verb = *sailed*)
>
> Jeff and his employees have reached a new pay agreement. (subjects = *Jeff* and *his employees*, verb = *have reached*)
>
> Gabrielle fixed the dripping tap and ordered a water tank. (subject = *Gabrielle*, verbs = *fixed* and *ordered*)

Note that one of these sentences has two subjects and one has two verbs, but each expresses one main idea.

Here are a few examples of sentences with more than one clause:

> SENTENCE: Bobo loves Luke, and she likes him to cook for her.
>
> CLAUSE 1: Bobo loves Luke (subject = *Bobo*, verb = *loves*)
>
> CLAUSE 2: she likes him to cook for her (subject = *she*, verb = *likes*)

SENTENCE: Tran had finished most of his homework, so his mother said that he could watch his favourite television show.

CLAUSE 1: Tran had finished most of his homework (subject = *Tran*, verb = *had finished*)

CLAUSE 2: his mother said that he could watch his favourite television show (subject = *his mother*, verb = *said*)

CLAUSE 3: that he could watch his favourite television show (subject= *he*, verb = *could watch*)

The second of the preceding sentences is a little odd. Clause 3 is actually part of clause 2. It isn't a misprint. Sometimes one clause is tangled up in another. It's called an *embedded* clause.

Main clauses

Some clauses are mature grown-ups. They live alone and make sense of the world. These clauses are called *independent* or *main* clauses. Other clauses are like middle-aged children who still live at home with their parents. These clauses aren't mature; they can't manage without support. These clauses are called *dependent* or *subordinate* clauses. (Both sets of terms are interchangeable.)

Both types of clauses, main and subordinate, have subject–verb pairs, but one big difference exists between them. Main clauses make complete sense on their own. Subordinate clauses don't.

Main clauses are okay by themselves. They make sense. They can manage alone. Writing too many main clauses in a row, however (as we just did in these introductory sentences), can make your paragraph sound choppy and dull.

You can combine main clauses with other main clauses to make more appealing sentences that add interest. *Coordinating conjunctions* are used to join main clauses to each other. When you do this, the message in each clause is of equal importance. (See the section 'Pairing equal ideas: Coordination', later in this chapter, for more about coordinating conjunctions.)

Here are some sentences to demonstrate the use of coordinating conjunctions:

SENTENCE: Bobo loves Luke *and* she likes him to cook their meals.

CLAUSE 1: Bobo loves Luke

COORDINATING CONJUNCTION: and

CLAUSE 2: she likes him to cook their meals

SENTENCE: She wanted duck à l'orange *but* he didn't know the recipe *nor* does he speak French.

CLAUSE 1: She wanted duck à l'orange

COORDINATING CONJUNCTION: but

CLAUSE 2: he didn't know the recipe

COORDINATING CONJUNCTION: nor

CLAUSE 3: does he speak French

Subordinate clauses

Subordinate clauses aren't okay by themselves because they don't make complete sense. They're not complete sentences.

When her father wasn't looking

Because Grandpa Griswald thrives on caffeine

Which she bought at the auction

To become complete sentences, subordinate clauses need the support of main clauses, which is why they're called subordinate: it means secondary or lower in rank. To make complete sense, subordinate clauses have to be attached to main clauses.

Subordinate clauses often function as (do the work of) adjectives or adverbs to the main clause, adding more information. They don't carry the main message.

Subordinate clauses add life and interest to a sentence; but, as with the friends crashing at your place (perhaps adding a little spice to the household), don't leave them alone! Disaster will strike. A subordinate clause all by itself is a grammatical crime — a sentence fragment. Stay tuned for more about sentence fragments later in this chapter.

The best sentences combine different elements in all sorts of patterns. In the following examples, the main clauses are combined with subordinate clauses to create longer, more interesting sentences:

Laura blasted Riley with her new water pistol when her father wasn't looking.

Because he thrives on caffeine, Grandpa Griswald was delighted to discover the packet of chocolate biscuits at the back of the cupboard.

Did she donate the watermelon, which she bought at the auction, to the school?

Coordination and Subordination

You need to organise your language so that others receive your message exactly as you intend it. The way you combine and connect ideas into chunks of meaning called sentences is an important part of clear communication. Without even knowing it, you use the skills of coordination and subordination whenever you use English, so try to put these skills in the front of your mind. That way you can use them on purpose.

Pairing equal ideas: Coordination

Good coordination training enables footballers to use both their right and left feet to kick with force and accuracy. *Coordinating ideas* in writing ensures that ideas of equal value are organised in logically connected main clauses and sentences. The *coordinating conjunctions* (*and, but, so, nor, yet, neither ... nor*) connect words and ideas of equal importance. In Chapter 7 we look at how we can also use semicolons, colons and conjuncts (including *therefore, thus, nevertheless*) to connect equal ideas. This process of connecting equal ideas is called *coordination*.

The following shows what happens with all three methods of coordination:

NO COORDINATION: Suddenly the rain stopped. The footpath sprang back to life with bustling bodies. I closed my umbrella. I began threading my way to school.

COORDINATION WITH COORDINATING CONJUNCTIONS: Suddenly the rain stopped *and* the footpath sprang back to life with bustling bodies, *so* I closed my umbrella *and* began threading my way to school. (Notice that the subject *I* has been omitted from the last idea because both parts of the sentence have exactly the same subject so you don't need to repeat it.)

COORDINATION WITH SEMICOLONS: Suddenly the rain stopped; the footpath sprang back to life with bustling bodies. I closed my umbrella; I began threading my way to school.

COORDINATION WITH CONJUNCTS: Suddenly the rain stopped; consequently, the footpath sprang back to life with bustling bodies. I closed my umbrella; thereafter, I began threading my way to school.

Note: The last two paragraphs would be unlikely to make it into print if they weren't examples in a grammar book. They're a little clunky, but the point is that each method of coordination creates a different style of paragraph and has a different effect.

Read them aloud and you can hear that using only coordinating conjunctions leads to a long, flat sentence. Using only semicolons jolts the reader along with its jumpiness, but hinges ideas closely. Using only conjuncts makes the paragraph sound so formal that it could have been written in a police statement. What works best with coordination is to mix and match the three methods to create the style you want. Like this:

VERSION 1: Suddenly the rain stopped; the footpath sprang back to life with bustling bodies. I closed my umbrella *and* began threading my way to school.

VERSION 2: Suddenly the rain stopped; consequently, the footpath sprang back to life with bustling bodies. I closed my umbrella *and then* I began threading my way to school.

VERSION 3: Suddenly the rain stopped *so* the footpath sprang back to life with bustling bodies. I closed my umbrella; I began threading my way to school.

These are just three possibilities. You can coordinate the ideas in many ways to create the exact meaning and impact you want.

Think about whether your piece is formal or informal. You're more likely to use conjuncts like *furthermore, moreover* or *nevertheless* in business writing than in a piece of fiction (unless you're creating a certain type of character and want to use words like this in the character's dialogue). And vary the connectors you choose. Don't restrict yourself to *and* if you mean *as well as, also, besides, too, on top of, along with* or *what's more.*

Coordinating unrelated or unequal ideas is like trying to make a sandwich with two differently sized pieces of bread. They don't fit together. Mismatches in sentences cause confusion because the ideas don't belong together. Also remember that stringing too many main clauses into just one sentence can bamboozle your reader because the way the ideas relate to each other becomes unclear. Finally, using only coordination can make your piece sound rather lacklustre. You're likely to engage your reader more effectively if you throw in some *subordination* — which is what we look at in the next section.

Demoting lesser ideas: Subordination

Not all ideas are equal. Some ideas outrank others and require *subordination*, which is the technique used to arrange the parts of a sentence that have different weight and importance. And here's something that probably won't shock you. Using *subordinating conjunctions* such as *because, since, as, unless, although* and *if* creates subordination of ideas.

As a general rule of subordination, the main idea goes in the *independent* or *main clause* of a sentence while the less significant information is relegated to the *dependent* or *subordinate clause*. Yes, using *subordinate clauses* achieves *subordination* in sentences. Who would have guessed? Here's an example of subordination at work. The main clauses are in italics:

Although she felt guilty, *Lucinda rejected Rashid's invitation to dinner.*

Lucinda felt guilty when she rejected Rashid's invitation to dinner.

The first example emphasises Lucinda's rejection of the invitation, while the second sentence stresses her guilt.

Subordination also involves using clauses beginning with pronouns such as *who, whom, whose, which, whatever, whichever* and *that* (called *relative clauses*). They carry information of lower rank than the idea expressed in a main clause. Sometimes, you can show that an idea isn't vitally important by shortening it from a clause to a phrase or even a single word. Here's how subordination works:

NO SUBORDINATION: I arrived back at the office. Rashid was waiting outside the lift. His face was red. He looked distressed. I was worried. Rashid is usually so calm.

SUBORDINATION WITH SUBORDINATING CONJUNCTIONS: I arrived back at the office *where* Rashid was waiting outside the lift. His face was red, *as if* he was distressed. I was worried *because* Rashid is usually so calm.

SUBORDINATION WITH RELATIVE CLAUSES: I arrived back at the office. Rashid, *whose face was red*, was waiting outside the lift. He was distressed, *which worried me*. Rashid is usually so calm. (Notice that the relative clauses are inside commas because they contain non-essential information that can be removed from the sentence.)

SUBORDINATION BY SHORTENING INFORMATION FROM CLAUSES: I arrived back at the office. Rashid, *usually so calm*, was waiting outside the lift, *red-faced and distressed*. I was worried. (The new descriptions are inside commas because they contain additional, non-essential information.)

The choices that you make about what information to put into the main clause and what to subordinate create different shades of meaning and emphasis. The order in which you put the information adds to this. Here are varied versions of the sample paragraph, each with a slightly different emphasis:

VERSION 1: *When* I arrived back at the office, Rashid, *who is usually calm*, was waiting outside the lift, *red-faced and distressed*. I was worried.

VERSION 2: I arrived back at the office *where* Rashid, *red-faced*, was waiting outside the lift. He was distressed, *which worried me because* he is usually so calm.

Be careful not to subordinate too many ideas in one sentence or your reader may lose track of the meaning. The following sentence, while grammatically correct, is confusing because it's too long:

> I was worried *when* I arrived back at the office *because* Rashid, *who is usually calm*, was waiting outside the lift, *red-faced and distressed*.

The main clause in this sentence is *I was worried* and all of the other information has been subordinated. Is that really the main idea of the sentence? And if it is, is your reader likely to see that it's the main point? Probably not, because it has been buried under an avalanche of extra information.

Creating logic with coordination and subordination

Good writing conveys precisely what you intend, no guessing or 'you know what I mean'-ing required. Using both coordination and subordination to connect sentence parts helps you to communicate clearly. By emphasising key ideas, subordinating less important information and balancing equal statements, you show your reader the exact relationships between the points you are making.

Here's an example of what happens when we mix the methods of connecting the ideas from the example paragraphs used in the two preceding sections on coordination and subordination. Remember, this is just one of many possible ways to connect the information. The subordinated ideas are in italics:

> Suddenly the rain stopped. The footpath sprang back to life with bustling bodies. *Closing my umbrella*, I began threading my way to school.
>
> *When I arrived back at the office*, Rashid, *red-faced and distressed* was waiting outside the lift. I was worried: Rashid is usually so calm.

Read the passage again and skip the bits in italics. See how only the extra bits of description are subordinated and the information the writer wants to emphasise are in the main clauses? The choice of punctuation also helps to isolate and connect the ideas. You've reached it: the intersection of grammar and style. Stride forth with confidence!

Having sentences of different lengths adds to the rhythm of what you write, which creates interest for your reader. Long sentences, with a mixture of subordinated ideas and coordinated elements (like this sentence) can slow down the pace of a piece of writing so that descriptions mimic the way our eyes or a movie camera move across a scene. Single idea sentences make a strong statement.

Alternate between long and short sentences. If you find you have written a string of long sentences, you can create more variety by cutting out wordy and repetitive phrases. You can also break some into shorter sentences. Be aware, however, that too many short sentences in a row can make your writing sound jerky and disconnected.

Use long sentences where you need to convey a lot of information or you want to describe something in detail. Use short sentences to make important points.

Considering Sentence Fragments

A sentence is not fully formed if it consists of only a phrase or a dependent clause. These are sometimes called *sentence fragments*. Here are some sentence fragment examples:

- Entering the room
- Because Shelley was so good at English
- Setsuko, who had lost her wallet
- As if by magic

Now here are fully formed sentences based on these fragments:

- Entering the room, she turned on the light.
- Because Shelley was so good at English, she won the prize.
- Setsuko, who had lost her wallet, could not catch the train home.
- The book rose into the air, as if by magic.

Fragmented subject–verb pair

Listen to a conversation. People rarely speak in complete sentences. Consider the following:

Where did you get that mud cake? (complete sentence)

From the cafe next door. (fragment: no subject or verb; needs *It came from the cafe next door* to be complete)

Looks delicious. (fragment: no subject; needs *It* looks delicious)

Sentence fragments often occur because the sentence doesn't have a complete subject–verb pair. (Remember them? Refer to 'You Complete Me: Subject and Verb Pairs', earlier in this chapter, for the details.)

Fragmented ideas

Another common type of incomplete sentence occurs when only part of an idea is communicated. If the first word is something like *and, but* or *because* (which are conjunctions), what follows is probably only half an idea. Conjunctions work like glue: they bind things together. Frequently, these words are used to combine two (or more) complete sentences (with two or more complete thoughts) into one longer sentence:

> Lucinda's mother was extremely thirsty, *but* she didn't like chamomile tea *and* that was all Ms Stakes was offering her.

The example contains three sentences, joined by a *but* and an *and*:

> Lucinda's mother was extremely thirsty. She didn't like chamomile tea. That was all Ms Stakes was offering her.

If you begin your sentence with a conjunction, what you're communicating may well fit the definition of a sentence (because it contains a subject–verb pair), but it can still be considered incomplete. Why? Because it only conveys part of the meaning. It's part of a longer sentence. Let's look at that incomplete sentence:

> Because it only conveys part of the meaning. (subject–verb pair = *it conveys*)

The subject–verb pair is present, but the idea is not complete. What's missing from this sentence is the first half. It's actually the end of the complete, longer sentence:

> It can still be considered incomplete because it only conveys part of the meaning.

It used to be a crime punishable by death to begin a sentence with a conjunction. Nowadays, writers commonly break this 'rule' and they don't spontaneously combust. But their computers probably caution them with the message 'Fragment (consider revising)' whenever they do it. Squiggly lines aplenty would draw attention to both of the following italicised groups of words:

> Marlo adores string concertos. *And plays violin.* (fragment)

> Marlo adores string concertos. *And she plays violin.* (incomplete sentence)

This is further proof that those bossy little grammar checkers are nowhere near as clever as we are. We know that the first example is a *fragment* of a sentence because it does not have a subject–verb pair. Who *plays*? No idea. However, the second example has the correct subject–verb pair *she plays*. If we remove the conjunction, a complete and correct sentence remains: *She plays violin.* See the difference? So the second example, although an incomplete sentence, is not a sentence fragment.

That said, beginning a sentence with a coordinating conjunction is frowned upon in formal writing. So how do you revise your conjunction-caused incomplete sentence? Any of several ways is possible. You could

- ✔ Try putting the sentences together with the conjunction as the connector.
- ✔ Remove the conjunction.
- ✔ Completely reword the sentence.
- ✔ Create a stronger emphasis by using a different kind of connecting word such as *additionally, also, as well as, however, on the other hand* or *whereas.*

Remember, too, that the other reason your computer may highlight a sentence fragment is that the sentence lacks a subject–verb pair. To revise such sentences, you need to provide the missing piece of the pair, or perhaps even add a subject–verb pair.

Revise the following to eliminate any sentence fragments.

> Carmine often arrives late. Having never provided an acceptable reason. And the person working the previous shift is frequently inconvenienced.

Answer: You have several acceptable ways to revise the given passage. So if your answer isn't exactly the same as ours, don't stress. The important thing is that you realise that 'sentence' two qualifies as a fragment because it lacks a subject–verb pair. Who is doing the *having*? *Carmine* — so the second idea needs to be connected to the first idea because they share the same subject. You should also have detected that 'sentence' three also fits into the fragment category because it begins with the coordinating conjunction *and.* So, your revised version could be something like: *Carmine often arrives late but has never provided an acceptable reason. The person working the previous shift is frequently inconvenienced.*

Proposing Relationships: Prepositions

As we mention in Chapter 1, prepositions are unassuming but important contributors to the language game. In this section, we explain everything you always wanted to know about prepositions but hoped you wouldn't have to ask.

Understanding how prepositions work

In Chapter 1, we cover how two nouns — 'wombat' and 'book' — can be connected. (Remember that a *noun* is a word for a person, place, thing or idea.) The book could be *about* the wombat, *by* the wombat, *behind* the wombat, *in front of* the wombat, *under* the wombat, or maybe just *near* the wombat.

The italicised words can't stand alone. They need to come in front of a noun or noun equivalent. That's why they're called *prepositions*. They're positioned before a noun — *pre* + *position*. Get it? This group of words relates a noun or a noun equivalent to another word in the sentence. Here's a list of some common prepositions.

about	as far as	due to	over
above	because of	during	past
according to	before	except	since
across	behind	for	through
after	below	from	towards
against	beneath	in	underneath
along	beside	in front of	until
amid	between	instead of	up
among	beyond	like	upon
around	by	of	with
apart from	concerning	off	within
at	down	on	without

Prepositions and objects

As we cover in the preceding section, prepositions never travel alone; they're always with a partner that completes them, an object. In the examples in the preceding section, the object of each preposition is 'wombat'. Just to get all the annoying terminology over with at once, a *prepositional phrase* consists of a preposition and its object. The object of a preposition is always a noun or noun equivalent. So it can be a pronoun, or perhaps a noun group. (A *pronoun* is a word that takes the place of a noun, like *he* for *Edgar* and so forth.)

Here's an example:

In the excitement, Buzza spilt his lemonade on Ando's little bald head.

This sentence has two prepositions: *in* and *on. Excitement* is the object of the preposition *in*, and the noun group *Ando's little bald head* is the object of the preposition *on*. (The noun *head* is the bare object — in both the grammatical and the literal sense of the word!)

So what do you get when you put the preposition back in front of the object and add the two together? That combination of words is the prepositional phrase. (A *phrase* is a group of words that has meaning but does not have a verb. And, not surprisingly, a prepositional phrase is a phrase that starts with a preposition.) Check out these prepositional phrases:

in spite of *the rain*

in spite of *drenching rain*

in spite of *the accurately predicted rain*

in spite of *such intensely annoying persistent rain*

Different from yours

What do you think? Is my point of view *different from* yours, *different to* yours or *different than* yours? Answer: It depends where you come from. In the United States, you would probably choose *different than* for speaking and *different from* for writing. In the UK, you'd be most likely to use *different from* with the occasional *different to*. So what about Australians? Basically, in Australia, you're likely to hear all three, but you can discard *different than*. It's frowned upon by those in the grammatical know (like you). You can use either of the other choices in casual language without fear of losing your credibility but, if you want to avoid offending anyone, choose *different from*. So, this rule is no *different from* any other; it's plagued by exceptions!

Each phrase is talking about the noun *rain* (the bare object), but to refer to the whole noun group as the object of the preposition makes more sense — otherwise, you're left with stray words like *the* and *accurately predicted* and no easy way to describe what they're doing. That's the beauty of functional grammar (yes, beauty most certainly *is* in the eye of the beholder). Functional grammar explains how words fit together in a logical way.

Questions that identify the objects of the prepositions

All objects — of a verb or of a preposition — answer the questions *whom?* or *what?* To find the object of a preposition, ask *whom?* or *what?* after the preposition.

In this sentence are two prepositional phrases:

> Mildred realised that the mouse under her bed had escaped from the snake's bowl.

The first preposition is *under*. Under what? *Under her bed. Her bed* is the object of the preposition *under*. The second preposition is *from*. From what? *From the snake's bowl. The snake's bowl* is the object of the preposition *from*.

What is the object of the preposition in this sentence?

> Nurse Oduwole knew that Inspector Barker was looking into her old English teacher's death.

Answer: *Death* is the object of the preposition *into*. When you ask the questions — into whom? or what? — the answer is the noun group *her old English teacher's death*. The bare object is the noun *death*.

Why do I need to know this?

When you're checking subject–verb pairs, you need to identify and then ignore the prepositional phrases. Why? Because the prepositional phrases are distractions. If you don't ignore them, you may end up matching the verb to the wrong word. You may also find sometimes, when you ask yourself the questions to find an adjective or an adverb, the answer is a prepositional phrase. Don't panic. A prepositional phrase may do the same job as an adjective or adverb. (See Chapter 6 for more on adjectives and adverbs.)

A prepositional phrase doesn't do the job of a preposition when it's at work in sentences. So, prepositional phrases are also referred to as either *adjectival phrases* or *adverbial phrases*, because these groups of words actually do the work of an adjective or an adverb in a sentence. Have a look at these:

> Harley ate a *large* meal. (*Large* is an adjective modifying the noun *meal.*)

> Harley ate a meal *of immense proportions*. (*Of immense proportions* is an adjectival phrase modifying the noun *meal.*)

Harley chewed *noisily.* (*Noisily* is an adverb modifying the verb *chewed.*)

Harley chewed *with alarming passion.* (*With alarming passion* is an adverbial phrase modifying the verb *chewed.*)

So you can think of prepositional phrases as being like people who have both a name from their birth-culture and an Anglicised name. Both names are part of their identity, and each can be used in particular situations.

You can set your computer to warn you if you have more than three prepositional phrases in a row. You need to consider revising such a sentence because it may be confusing for your reader, like this example:

The house *on the corner* (1) *of the street* (2) *near the school* (3) *in our neighbourhood* (4) burned down last night.

You could revise the sentence several ways to make it clearer, but here's one example to get you started:

The corner house near our local school burned down last night.

Ending a sentence with a preposition

You may have been told that ending a sentence with a preposition is unacceptable, based on the logic that a word called a *preposition* must *pre*-position something. Some people argue that, by definition, a preposition must come in front of a noun or noun equivalent. So it is not acceptable for the last word of a sentence to be a preposition. Well, let's test their theory:

Tell me what you are thinking *about.*

Tell me *about* what you are thinking.

Guess what? Both sentences are acceptable. And here's why. Sometimes, a preposition acts as an additional word to make a two-part verb. When this happens, the preposition becomes part of a verb group and is not acting as a preposition at all. In the preceding sample sentence, the preposition *about* is more closely related to the verb group *are thinking* than it is to any of the noun equivalents in the sentence. A difference in meaning exists between *to think about* (to consider) and *to think* (to believe). Hence, you have no logical reason not to finish the sentence with the offending word, because it's part of a compound verb or verb group, and verbs are fine at the end of a sentence.

Stopping Safely: Finishing a Sentence

When you speak, your body language, silences and tone act as punctuation marks. You wriggle your eyebrows, wave your hands about, stop at significant moments and raise your tone when you ask a question. When you write, you can't raise an eyebrow or stop for a dramatic moment. No-one hears your tone of voice. That's why grammar uses *endmarks*. The endmarks take the place of live communication and tell your reader how to 'hear' the words correctly. Plus, you need endmarks to close your sentences legally. Your choices are the full stop (.), question mark (?) and exclamation mark (!). The following examples show how to use endmarks correctly.

The full stop is for ordinary statements, declarations and commands:

> I can't dance.
>
> I refuse to dance.
>
> Don't make me dance.

The question mark is for questions:

> Why are you torturing me with this song?
>
> How can you bear it?
>
> Don't you care about noise pollution?

The exclamation mark is used (sparingly) to add a little drama to sentences that would otherwise end in full stops:

> I don't dance!
>
> I absolutely positively refuse to do it!
>
> Oh, turn it off!

If your sentence ends with an abbreviation, let the full stop that you use after the abbreviation do double duty. Don't add another one:

> WRONG: Please bring a pillow, sleeping bag, teddy bear, bed socks etc..
>
> RIGHT: Please bring a pillow, sleeping bag, teddy bear, bed socks etc.

Ellipsis points (. . .) are used to show that something is missing. They can be used in the middle of a sentence to show that words have been left out, or at the end of a sentence if the words trail off to nothingness. An ellipsis is always just three dots — you don't need to add a full stop if the ellipsis comes at the end of the sentence. (See Chapter 10 for more on ellipses.)

Can you punctuate this extract correctly?

How am I going to tell Maria that I don't like her cooking she has tried so hard I know she wants me to tell her how wonderful this meal is and I really don't want to hurt her feelings should I tell a white lie oh dear maybe I could just

Answer: How am I going to tell Maria that I don't like her cooking? She has tried so hard. I know she wants me to tell her how wonderful this meal is, and I really don't want to hurt her feelings. Should I tell a white lie? Oh dear! Maybe I could just . . .

Chapter 5

Peaking with Pronouns

Many long years ago, in a land where men were chivalrous and ladies all wore dresses, one would always place oneself last in the sentence, speaking thusly: 'Wouldst anyone care to come a-wassailing with Lord Jagger, Sir Bob and I?'

The people of the kingdom were committing unpardonable sins in the use of pronouns. So, their error was passed down the lines of their descendants verily unto the modern day.

Yes, choosing the correct pronoun can be tricky, even for those who can wield a sword or ride side-saddle. *Pronouns* are words that substitute for nouns. English has many different types of pronoun, each governed by its own set of rules. In this chapter, we concentrate on how to avoid the most common errors associated with this class of words.

Matching Nouns and Pronouns

Pronouns stand in for other words. So, to choose the appropriate pronoun, you must consider the word that the pronoun is replacing (which is called the pronoun's *antecedent* — a name meaning 'going before'). Here's a look at how this works:

> Millie Magpie fed *her* chicks the delicious sausage *she* stole from the barbeque below *her* nest. (The pronouns *her* and *she* stand in for the antecedent *Millie Magpie*.)

Johnno, *who* hates fruit, tried to convince *his* health-conscious mum to buy soft drink for the birthday party. (The pronouns *who* and *his* stand for the antecedent *Johnno*.)

You should be able to replace the pronoun with its antecedent (or the antecedent with the pronoun) without changing the meaning of the sentence.

Avoiding Vague Pronoun Use

The best way to remain clear in your use of pronouns is to keep the pronoun and its antecedent close to each other. Vague use of pronouns can confuse your reader or listener. Check this out:

Costa had hay fever. He pulled out his handkerchief. He blew his nose. Yasmin had given it to him — the love of his life. He was terrified of losing her. He sniffed. It was always worse when he walked through the park. She was a treasure.

This example has more than one problem. *Yasmin* is too far from *she*, and we have no idea what's worse when Costa walks through the park, his hay fever or his emotional state. (And did she really give him his *nose*?) Here's one possible revision:

Costa had hay fever, and it was always worse when he walked through the park. He pulled out his handkerchief. Yasmin — the love of his life — had given it to him. She was a treasure. He was terrified of losing her. He sniffed and blew his nose.

Now the antecedents and pronouns are closer to each other. Much better!

While it's true that a pronoun is more likely to be understood if it's placed near the word it replaces, position isn't always enough, especially if more than one antecedent is possible. Look at this sentence:

Lucinda told her mother that she was out of cash.

Who's out of cash? The sentence has one pronoun (*she*) and two nouns (*Lucinda* and *Lucinda's mother*). *She* could refer to either of them. The antecedent is not clear. The best way to clarify the meaning of a pronoun is to make sure that each pronoun represents only one easily identifiable antecedent. If readers can interpret the sentence in more than one way, rewrite it:

> Lucinda was out of cash so she told the sad tale to her mother.

or

> Lucinda saw that her mother was out of cash and told her so.

What does this sentence mean?

> Sandy and her sister went to Lucinda's birthday party, but she didn't have a good time.

>> **A.** Sandy didn't have a good time.

>> **B.** Sandy's sister didn't have a good time.

>> **C.** Lucinda didn't have a good time.

Answer: Who knows? Rephrase the sentence, unless you're talking to someone who was at the party and knows that Sandy loved every minute of it and Sandy's sister left wearing a large grin, just after Lucinda broke both a bottle of expensive perfume and the heel on her Jimmy Choos, and that was before the cops arrived. If your listener knows all that, the sentence is fine. If not, here are a few possible rewrites:

> Sandy and her sister went to Lucinda's party. Lucinda didn't have a good time.

> Lucinda didn't have a good time at her own birthday party, even though Sandy and Sandy's sister were there.

> Sandy and her sister went to Lucinda's party, but Lucinda didn't have a good time.

Choosing Singular and Plural Pronouns

All pronouns are either singular or plural. *Singular* pronouns replace singular nouns, which are those that name *one* person, place, thing or idea. *Plural* pronouns replace plural nouns — those that name *more than one* person, place, thing or idea. Logical enough, right? So just to make things crystal clear, Table 5-1 lists some common singular and plural pronouns.

Table 5-1	Common Singular and Plural Pronouns
Singular	*Plural*
I	we
me	us
myself	ourselves
you	you
yourself	yourselves
he/she/it	they/them
himself/herself/itself	themselves
who	who
which	which
that	that

Pairing Pronouns with Collective Nouns

Collective nouns (*orchestra, committee, team, squad, army, class* and the like) refer to groups and can present a problem when choosing the right pronouns (and verbs).

Collective nouns exist because these groups often act as a unit, doing the same thing at the same time. If that's the case, treat the noun as singular and make sure that the pronouns that refer to it are also singular. Like this:

> The audience rises and is ready to leave as soon as the concert ends.

So, if the audience is a unit, would the audience clap *its* hands or *their* hands? Let's see:

> The audience rises and is ready to leave as soon as *it* has finished clapping *its* hands. (Oh dear.)

The audience doesn't share two big hands. You can safely assume that 99.7 per cent of audience members have two individual hands each. So how do you fix the problem? Dump the collective noun and substitute the plural *members of the audience*:

> The members of the audience rise and *are* ready to leave as soon as *they have* finished clapping *their* hands.

Members is now the subject. *Members* is plural, so the verbs (*are, have*) and pronouns (*they, their*) are all plural too.

To sum up the general rules on pronouns that refer to groups:

- ✔ Treat collective nouns as singular if the group is acting as a unit.

- ✔ Some collective nouns may take singular or plural pronouns and verbs, but do not mix the two for the same collective noun — especially not in a single sentence.

- ✔ If the members of the group are acting as individuals, you can use a plural verb, but it's better to switch the collective noun for a plural noun.

No matter what you might see (or hear) on websites, in advertisements, on billboards and even in mail, company names are always singular and so must take singular pronouns and verbs. Yes, even if the company name ends with an *s*, and even if the company employs half the planet. For example:

Eccentric Electronics is moving *its* operation.

Catherine's Cookies has crumbled and closed *its* doors.

Which of the following are correct?

A. The class will hold its annual fun run next week. The class always enjoy their day out.

B. The class will hold its annual fun run next week. The class always enjoys its day out.

C. The class will hold their annual fun run next week. The class always enjoy their day out.

D. The annual class fun run will take place next week. The students always enjoy their day out.

Answer: Answers B, C and D are all correct. The problem collective noun is *class*. Answer A is definitely wrong because it begins by treating *class* as singular (*its* picnic) but then switches to plural (*enjoy their* day out). Answer B treats *class* as singular. Answer C treats it as plural. They're both correct. Experts may not like your choice, but they won't argue with it as long as you're consistent. But option D is the best: it avoids using *class* as a noun (it's an adjective in *annual class fun run*) and uses *students* instead in the second sentence.

Selecting Pronouns as Subjects

The subject is the person or thing that is 'doing' the action of the verb (or 'being' the verb if it's a linking verb). (For more on locating the subject, refer to Chapter 2.) The *object* in a sentence is the person or thing that receives the action of the verb.

You can't do much wrong when you have the actual name of a person, place or thing as the subject — in other words, a noun — but pronouns are another story.

The following can help you to remember which are the only legal subject pronouns (and which are the object pronouns).

Subject Pronouns	Object Pronouns
I, you, he, she, it	me, you, him, her, it
we, they	us, them
who, whoever	whom, whomever

Here are some examples of pronouns as the subject of a sentence:

Actually, *I* did once ride a horse side-saddle. (*I* is the subject of the verb *did*.)

Whoever marries Damian next should have her head examined. (*Whoever* is the subject of the verb *marries*.)

Matching more than one subject

Most people can manage one subject, but sentences with two or more subjects (*compound subjects*) can be tricky. For example, you often hear otherwise grammatically correct speakers say things like

Him and *me* are going to get some fish and chips.

Damian and *me* had met before.

See the problem? In the first example, the verb *are going* expresses the action. To find the subject, ask *who* or *what are going?* The answer right now is *him and me are going*, but *him* isn't a subject pronoun. Neither is *me*. Here's the correct version:

He and *I* are going to get some carrots and celery. (We couldn't resist correcting the nutritional content too.)

In the second example, the action — the verb — is *had met*. Who or *what had met?* The answer, as it is now, is *Damian and me*. *Me* is not a legal subject pronoun. The correct version is

Damian and *I* had met before.

A good way to check your pronoun use in sentences with more than one subject is to look at each one separately. You may have to adjust the verb a bit when you're speaking about one subject instead of two, but the principle is the same. If the pronoun doesn't work as a solo subject, it isn't right as part of a pair either. Here's an example:

> ORIGINAL SENTENCE: *Lucinda* and *me* went shopping in the sales yesterday.
>
> CHECK: *Lucinda* went shopping yesterday. Verdict: no problem.
>
> CHECK: *Me* went shopping in the sales yesterday. Verdict: problem. Substitute *I.*
>
> CHECK THE REVISED VERSION: *I* went shopping in the sales yesterday. Verdict: that's better.
>
> COMBINED, CORRECTED SENTENCE: *Lucinda* and *I* went shopping in the sales yesterday.

Selecting pronouns as objects

In the preceding sections, we've concentrated on subject pronouns — pronouns that perform the action of the verb — but now it's time to focus on the receiver of the sentence's action — the object. Specifically, it's time to examine *object pronouns.* (If the verb is the engine and the subject is the driver in a sentence, the object or the complement are common (but not always essential) parts of the car. They *complete* the sentence.) Pronouns that may legally function as objects include *me, you, him, her, it, us, them, whom* and *whomever.*

Here are some examples of object pronouns, all in italics:

> Dad took *us* to the new movie despite its dreadful reviews. (*Took* is the verb; *Dad* is the subject; *us* is the object.)
>
> Someone sent *me* a very obscure *text message.* (*Sent* is the verb; *someone* is the subject; *text message* and *me* are objects.)

Owning Possessive Pronouns

Possessive pronouns show (pause for a drum roll) *possession.* Not the head-spinning-around, projectile-vomiting kind of possession, but the kind where you own something. Check out the following:

> Sure that *his* phone had beeped *its* last beep, Shane shopped for a new one.

The possessive pronouns in this example show that the beep belongs to the phone and the phone belongs to Shane.

Possessive pronouns also have singular and plural forms. You need to keep them straight. Table 5-2 helps you identify each type.

Table 5-2	Singular and Plural Possessive Pronouns
Singular	*Plural*
my	our
mine	ours
your	your
yours	yours
his/her/hers/one's	their/theirs
its	their
whose	whose

Putting an apostrophe into the possessive pronoun *its* is a very common error, and your computer often highlights it for you to check. *It's* does not mean *belongs to it*. *It's* means *it is*. Always. Without exception. *It's* and *its* work like this:

> My computer exploded and *its* RAM is more random than ever before. (belonging to *it*)
>
> *It's* raining data in here. (it is)
>
> *It's* been a while since I backed up the hard drive. (it has)

One's is the only possessive pronoun that ever has an apostrophe, and unless you live in that quaint land referred to at the start of this chapter, you probably never use *one's* anyway.

Reflecting on Reflexive Pronouns

In this era of self-interest, *reflexive pronouns* (also called the *-self pronouns*) get quite a workout. Just as a mirror reflects an image back to you, so a *reflexive pronoun* reflects another word (a noun or noun equivalent) used earlier in the sentence. The reflexive pronouns are *myself, yourself, himself, herself, itself, oneself, ourselves, yourselves* and *themselves*. Here are some of them at work:

> Lucinda's parents blamed *themselves* for her selfishness. (*themselves* refers back to the noun group *Lucinda's parents*)

> She behaves *herself* only with difficulty. (*herself* refers back to the pronoun *she*)

The word to which any pronoun refers back is called its *antecedent*. With *reflexive pronouns*, the antecedent is always the subject of a verb.

A second legitimate use for these self-confident pronouns is to emphasise or focus on something specific about the word to which the reflexive pronoun refers back (its antecedent). Some picky grammarians call this same group of pronouns *intensive pronouns* because they intensify the point being made about the subject of the verb, like this:

> Tex *himself* will be playing guitar on my new song. (And we all know what a hot guitarist Tex is.)

> I mowed the grass *myself*. (Even though I've never done it before but I was sick of waiting for you to do it.)

Some people consistently use reflexive pronouns incorrectly (probably because they think it sounds more formal).

> WRONG: Please address your response to Charlotte and *myself*.

> RIGHT: Please address your response to Charlotte and *me*.

Sentences such as the preceding example require a pronoun from the object list (*address your response* to whom? *address your response* to me) not a reflexive pronoun.

In the paper it says

Are you writing about literature or what's in the paper? If so, beware of *it* and *they*. Some common errors follow those pronouns. Check out these examples:

> In *Hamlet*, it says that Claudius is a murderer.

Oh really? What does *it* mean? The play can't speak, and the author of the play (Shakespeare) is a *who*. Actually, in *Hamlet*, the ghost says that Claudius is a murderer, but even the ghost is a *he*. In other words, *it* has no antecedent. Reword the sentence:

> In *Hamlet*, Claudius is a murderer.

> The ghost in Hamlet reveals that Claudius is a murderer.

Here's another example:

> In today's paper *they* say that more and more people want to drop Shakespeare's

plays from the curriculum because they can't understand the language.

Who is *they*? Perhaps the authors of an article, but the sentence doesn't make that clear. It's possible that the author of the sentence thinks *they* is a good all-purpose pronoun for talking about anonymous or nameless authors. In other words, the antecedent of *they* is 'I don't know and I really don't care.' Wrong! The antecedent of *they* must be a real, identifiable group of people. Some possible corrections include:

> Today's paper reports that more and more people want to drop Shakespeare's plays from the school curriculum because students can't understand the language.

> In today's paper, education critic I M Wellred says that Shakespeare's plays should be dropped from the curriculum because teachers cannot understand the language.

This, That and the Other

One pronoun may refer to one noun. A plural pronoun may refer to more than one noun. But no pronoun may refer to a whole sentence or a whole paragraph. Consider the following:

> Rob's friend Isolde likes to arrive at school around 11 each day because she thinks that getting up earlier than 10 is barbaric. The principal, not surprisingly, thinks that arriving at school over two hours late each day is not a good idea. *This* is a problem.

This certainly is a problem, and not because of Isolde's sleeping habits or the principal's beliefs. *This* is a problem because *this* is a pronoun but the antecedent of the word *this* is unclear. What does *this* mean? The fact that

Isolde arrives around 11? That Isolde thinks getting up before 10 is out of the question? Or that the principal and Isolde are not, to put it mildly, in sync? Or all of the above?

The writer probably intends *this* to refer to *all of the above*. Unfortunately, *all of the above* is not a good answer to the question, 'What does the pronoun mean?' Thus:

> WRONG: The red dye looked horrible, and the new straightening iron had singed her hair. *This* persuaded Bobo to use a professional hairdresser in future.

> WHY IT'S WRONG: *This* is referring to the 14 words of the preceding sentence, not to one noun.

> RIGHT: Because the red dye looked horrible and the new straightening iron had singed her hair, Bobo decided to use a professional hairdresser in future.

> WHY IT'S RIGHT: Eliminating *this* eliminates the problem.

Part II
Adding Detail and Avoiding Common Errors

Top Five Punctuation Marks

- **Commas:** Commas (,) break your sentences into chunks to help you communicate your exact meaning. The key is to put the commas where they help the reader to see and hear the sense of the sentence.

- **Apostrophes:** These marks (') can be used to shorten words, to show ownership and (only sometimes) to form plurals.

- **Semicolons:** Semicolons (;) can join one complete sentence to another. They're a stronger piece of punctuation than a comma, but not as strong as a full stop. Think of a semicolon as a hinge connecting two sentences.

- **Colons:** Colons (:) also show up when a simple comma isn't strong enough to connect ideas. A colon draws attention to the material that follows it, and is used to introduce information that develops or explains the words preceding the colon.

- **Hyphens and dashes:** Hyphens (-) are short dashes used to link two words or word parts so that they do the work of one word, and are also used to form compound words. Dashes (– or —) indicate extra information and can be used singularly or in pairs. A pair of dashes shows a strong interruption from the rest of the sentence.

In this part ...

- ✔ Express yourself with flair by adding descriptions with adjectives and adverbs.
- ✔ Understand the nails, nuts and bolts of writing — including commas, semicolons, colons, hyphens and dashes.
- ✔ Work out when you need an apostrophe — and when you don't.
- ✔ Capitalise with precision, and know when using numerals is best.
- ✔ Discover the best ways to include someone else's words in your writing.

Chapter 6

Modifying with Adjectives and Adverbs

*W*ith the right nouns (names of people, places, things or ideas) and verbs (action or being words) you can create a pretty solid, but basic, sentence. In this chapter, we explain the two main types of descriptive words of the English language — *adjectives* and *adverbs*. We also show you how to use each correctly to add meaning and interest to your sentence.

You may be wondering whether these words really matter. If you've ever wished that a writer would stop describing the scenery and get on with the story, you probably think that descriptive words just hold up the action. But sometimes they can be the key to expressing your meaning. If you don't believe that, take a look at this sentence:

> Lucinda was sauntering through Westfield when the sight of a Ferragamo Paradiso paralysed her.

Would you understand this sentence? What do you need to know in order to make sense of it? Apart from the meaning of words like *saunter* (which you could look up in a dictionary if you weren't sure what it meant), you'd need some background information. For example:

✔ Westfield is a shopping centre. (You probably do know that.)

✔ Ferragamo is an expensive shoe label. (Maybe you know that.)

✔ A Paradiso is a type of shoe. (You couldn't know that because we made it up.)

It would also help to know that Lucinda is obsessed with shoes. If you knew all this, or if you have a good imagination and the ability to use context clues when reading, you probably understood it.

But what if you didn't know all this to start with? That's when descriptions can be useful. Here's version two:

> *Shoe-obsessed* Lucinda was sauntering through *consumer-oriented* Westfield when the sight of a *fashionable, green, high-heeled evening* sandal with the *ultra-chic* Ferragamo label paralysed her.

Okay, it's overloaded a bit, but you get the point. The descriptive words help to clarify the meaning of the sentence, particularly for the fashion-challenged.

Now that you realise that descriptions can be essential to the meaning of a sentence, we know you're dying to find out more. Read on.

Adding Meaning with Adjectives

An *adjective* is a descriptive word that *modifies*, or adds more detail about, a noun or a pronoun. It adds information about number, colour, type and other qualities to your sentence.

Where do adjectives hang out? Most of the time you find them in front of a noun (the one the adjective is describing), but they roam about a bit. You may find them after the noun or after a pronoun (when they're describing the pronoun). And sometimes you find them connected to their noun by a linking verb. We look at all these ways of using adjectives in turn.

Uncovering adjectives

To find adjectives, go to the words they modify (nouns and pronouns). Find the noun and ask these questions:

- ✔ How many?
- ✔ Which one?
- ✔ What kind?

Take a look at this sentence:

> Magneto placed the three short red wires in his new invention.

You see three nouns: *Magneto, wires* and *invention*. You can't find answers to the questions *How many Magnetos? Which Magneto?* or *What kind of Magneto?* The sentence doesn't give that information; no adjectives describe *Magneto*.

But try the three questions on *wires* and *invention* and you do come up with something. How many wires? Answer: *Three. Three* is an adjective. What kind of wires? Answer: *Red* and *short. Red* and *short* are adjectives. The same goes for *invention*. What kind? Answer: *New. New* is an adjective.

His also answers one of the questions. (Which invention? Answer: *His invention.) His* is working as an adjective, but *his* also belongs to the word class called pronouns. Some grammarians call *his* a pronoun and others call *his* an adjective. The more modern of us prefer to call it a *determiner* (a class of words that can be used to modify a noun instead of using *a* or *the*.) Whatever you call it, *his* functions in the same way in the sentence; it adds detail to a noun.

Find the adjectives in this sentence.

> Gentle Martin always has a kind word for everyone exhausted by training, even though he is tired and hungry too.

Answer: *Gentle* (describing *Martin*), *kind* (describing *word*), *exhausted* (describing *everyone*), *tired* and *hungry* (describing *he*).

Adding adjectives to nouns

The most common job for an adjective is adding to the meaning of a *noun* — describing a noun. Here are some sentences with the adjectives in italics:

> There is a *poisonous* snake on your shoulder.

> There is an *angry venomous* snake on your shoulder.

> There is a *rubber* snake on your shoulder.

All the adjectives are describing the noun *snake* and they're all in front of the noun. The second sentence has two adjectives and they're stuck together without anything connecting or separating them. In these three sentences, those little descriptive words certainly make a difference. They give you information that you would really like to have. See how diverse and powerful adjectives can be?

Now here's an example with the adjectives after the noun:

> Kyle, *sore* and *tired*, pleaded with Sandy to release him from the headlock she had placed on him.

Sore and *tired* tell you about *Kyle*. Note that when more than one adjective is used after a noun they need to be joined by an *and*. You can't just say *Kyle, sore tired* (*sore* seems to be describing *tired* rather than *Kyle*). If you use more than two adjectives, you should punctuate them like a list. Here's an example using three adjectives after the noun:

> Kyle, *sore, tired and thirsty*, pleaded with Sandy to release him from the headlock she had placed on him.

If you can put the word 'and' between the adjectives, you can separate them with a comma. You could have *sore and tired and thirsty*. But look at this example:

> Kris closed the *large, steel garage* door onto the bonnet of Eva's new car.

You could say *a large and steel garage door* but you wouldn't say *a large and steel and garage door*. *Garage* is not just describing *door*, the adjective is actually defining the noun. *Garage door* is a particular type of door, not just a description of the door. The last comma has been omitted from the list of adjectives in the last sentence because *garage* is defining *door*.

In fact, defining adjectives couple so closely with their noun partners that they almost form a compound noun. That's how language changes. A defining adjective and a noun get so attached to each other that they decide to link up with a hyphen. Pretty soon they can't bear that distance either, and so they drop their hyphen and become permanently attached as a single word. For example, *back yard* morphed into *back-yard* before reinventing itself as *backyard*.

Adding adjectives to pronouns

Adjectives can also modify or tell you more about *pronouns* — they can describe pronouns (words that substitute for nouns):

> There's something *strange* on your shoulder. (The adjective *strange* describes the pronoun *something*.)

> Everyone *conscious* at the end of the play made a quick exit. (The adjective *conscious* describes the pronoun *everyone*.)

As you can see, these adjectives usually go after their pronouns.

Using adjectives with linking verbs

Adjectives may also follow *linking verbs*, in which case they describe the subject of the sentence (which can, of course, be a noun or a pronoun). Linking verbs join two ideas, associating one with the other. They're like equals signs, equating the *subject* (which comes before the verb) with another idea that comes after the verb. (Refer to Chapter 2 for full details of linking verbs.)

Sometimes a linking verb joins the subject to an adjective (or a couple of adjectives):

> The afternoon appears *dull* because of the nuclear fallout from Uncle Winston's cigars. (The adjective *dull* describes the noun *afternoon*.)

> Now the car is *bent* and *sad*. (The adjectives *bent* and *sad* describe the noun *car*.)

You'll notice that an *and* appears between the adjectives *bent* and *sad* when they come after a linking verb (just as it does when two or more adjectives come *after* a noun).

When adjectives are positioned before a noun (*the right choice*) they're called *attributive* adjectives. When they follow a linking verb (*the choice is right*), they're called *predicative* adjectives. Most adjectives in English can be used in both ways (like *right*), but some can't. For example, *alive* and *asleep* can't be used attributively — you can say *the children are asleep* and *the snake is alive* but not *the asleep children* or *the alive snake*. And *mere* and *latter* can't be used predicatively — you can say *a mere instant* and *the latter half* but not *the instant is mere* or *the half is latter*.

Describing with Adverbs

Adjectives aren't the only descriptive words. *Adverbs* are also descriptive words. These words modify the meaning of a verb, an adjective or another adverb. Check these out:

> The boss *regretfully* said no to Rashid's request for a raise.

> The boss *furiously* said no to Rashid's request for a raise.

> The boss *never* said no to Rashid's requests for a raise.

If you're Rashid, you care whether the word *regretfully, furiously* or *never* is in the sentence. *Regretfully, furiously* and *never* are all adverbs. Notice how adverbs add meaning in these sentences:

Ellie *sadly* sang Sia's latest song. (Perhaps Ellie is feeling sad or perhaps it's a sad song.)

Ellie sang Sia's latest song *reluctantly*. (Ellie doesn't want to sing this song or she doesn't feel like singing at all.)

Ellie *hoarsely* sang Sia's latest song. (Ellie has a cold.)

Ellie sang Sia's latest song *quickly*. (Ellie is in a hurry.)

Finding the adverb

Adverbs mostly modify verbs, giving more information about an action. Nearly all adverbs (enough so that you don't have to worry about the ones that fall through the cracks) answer one of these four questions:

- ✔ How?
- ✔ When?
- ✔ Where?
- ✔ Why?

To find the adverb, go to the verb and ask yourself the questions directly after the verb. (Refer to Chapter 2 for information on finding the verbs.) Look at this sentence:

'I've finally solved the mystery of the book,' said the sergeant quickly, as he was just going.

First, identify the verbs. Three are used: *solved, said* and *was going*. Then ask the questions. Solved when? Answer: *Finally. Finally* is an adverb. Solved how? Solved where? Solved why? No answers. Now for *said*. Said how? Answer: *Quickly. Quickly* is an adverb. Said where? Said when? Said why? No answers. And finally, *was going*. Was going how? No answer. Was going when? Answer: *Just. Just* is an adverb. Was going where? No answer. Was going why? No answer. The adverbs are *finally, quickly* and *just*.

Adverbs can be in lots of places in a sentence. If you're trying to find them, rely on the answer to your questions *how, when, where* and *why*, not the location of the word in the sentence. Similarly, a word may be an adverb in one sentence and something else in another sentence. Check these out:

Lucinda went *home* in a huff.

Home is where the heart is.

Home movies are Mildred's specialty.

In the first example, *home* tells you where Lucinda went, so *home* is an adverb in that sentence. In the second example, *home* is a place, so *home* is a noun in that sentence. In the third example, *home* is an adjective, telling you what kind of movies they are.

Using adverbs to describe adjectives and other adverbs

Adverbs also describe other descriptions, usually making the description more or less intense. (A description describing a description? Give me a break! But it's true.) Here's an example:

Nicole was extremely unhappy when Keith didn't phone her.

How unhappy? Answer: *Extremely unhappy. Extremely* is an adverb describing the adjective *unhappy*.

Sometimes the questions you pose to locate adjectives and adverbs are answered by more than one word in a sentence. In the previous example sentence, if you ask *Was when?* the answer is *when Keith didn't phone her*. Don't panic. These longer answers are just different forms of adjectives and adverbs.

Here's another example:

Nicole quite sensibly put it out of her mind and reorganised her bank accounts.

This time an adverb is describing another adverb. *Sensibly* is an adverb because it explains how Nicole *put*. In other words, *sensibly* describes the verb *put*. How sensibly? Answer: *Quite sensibly. Quite* is an adverb describing the adverb *sensibly*, which in turn describes the verb *put*.

In general, you don't need to worry too much about adverbs that describe adjectives or other adverbs; only a few errors are associated with this type of description. See 'Sorting adjective–adverb pairs' later in this chapter for some tips.

Distinguishing Between Adjectives and Adverbs

Does it matter whether a word is an adjective or an adverb? Some of the time, no. You've been talking and writing happily for a few years now, and you've likely spent very little time worrying about this issue. As a toddler, you demanded, 'I want a snack NOW.' You didn't know you were adding an adverb to your sentence. For that matter, you didn't know you were making a sentence. You were just hungry. But, some of the time, knowing the difference is helpful. In this section we tell you how to apply the *-ly* test to sort adjectives from adverbs, and how to decide between some commonly confused pairs of adjectives and adverbs.

Using the -ly test

Strictly is an adverb, and *strict* is an adjective. *Nicely* is an adverb, and *nice* is an adjective. *Generally* is an adverb, and *general* is an adjective. *Lovely* is a . . . gotcha! You were going to say *adverb*, right? Wrong. *Lovely* is an adjective. But you can use the *-ly* test for lots of adverbs. Just bear in mind that not all *-ly* words are adverbs and that lots of words (like *soon*, *now* and *fast*) are adverbs even though they don't end in *-ly*. The best way to tell if a word is an adverb is to ask the four adverb questions: *how*, *when*, *where* and *why*. If the word answers one of those questions, it's an adverb.

Identify the adjectives and adverbs in these sentences.

A. Thank him for the lovely presents he so kindly gave you yesterday.

B. Her knitting, folded neatly in her old work basket, will not be finished.

Answers: In sentence A, *lovely* is an adjective describing *presents*. *Kindly* is an adverb describing the verb *gave*, and *so* is an adverb describing the adverb *kindly*. *Yesterday* is an adverb describing when he *gave* the presents. In sentence B, *neatly* is an adverb describing the verb *folded*. *Old* and *work* are adjectives describing *basket*. *Not* is an adverb reversing the meaning of the verb *will be finished*. (And you can call *her* an adjective if you want to.)

Sorting adjective–adverb pairs

Time for some practice in choosing between adjectives and adverbs. As we cover in the preceding section, a lot of common adverbs are distinguished from their adjectives by the letters *-ly*:

> The crowd gave a *sudden* gasp when Miss Argentina tripped on her gown.

> Brad stopped *suddenly* when he saw Jennifer approaching.

Sudden is an adjective describing the noun *gasp*. *Suddenly* is an adverb describing how Brad *stopped* (a verb). Take a look at these examples (we begin with some easy pairs, to allow you to apply the *-ly* test):

> WRONG: Damian grins *casual* when he's bluffing.

> RIGHT: Damian grins *casually* when he's bluffing.

> WHY IT'S RIGHT: The adverb *casually* describes how Damian *grins*.

> ALSO RIGHT: Damian's *casual* grin gives him away every time.

> WHY IT'S ALSO RIGHT: The adjective *casual* describes the noun *grin*.

Don't stop now! Check these examples:

> WRONG: I did really *bad* on the test, Dad.

> RIGHT: I did really *badly* on the test, Dad.

> WHY IT'S RIGHT: The adverb *badly* describes how I *did* (a verb). Confusing *bad* and *badly* is a common error. But, as you can see, the *-ly* test works.

Remember: adjectives modify nouns or pronouns, and adverbs modify verbs, adjectives or other adverbs.

Chapter 7

Punctuation for Sense

. . . .

In This Chapter

▶ Putting commas in all the right places

▶ Understanding how semicolons join sentences and punctuate lists

▶ Using colons to introduce lists and explanations

▶ Differentiating between hyphens and dashes

▶ Knowing when to use brackets and how to punctuate them

. . . .

*Y*ou don't need to be a construction expert to know that a building requires more than steel, timber and bricks. A plethora of little things — nails, bolts, mortar, rivets — also complete the structure and make it strong. The same is true of good communication.

So in this chapter, we explain some of the rivets and bolts of writing: commas, semicolons, colons and dashes. (In Chapter 8, we cover another important rivet: apostrophes.) By the end of this chapter, you'll understand how punctuation is an essential part of the communication-building process.

Understanding the Point of Punctuation

Sentence boundaries are shown by punctuation. Capital letters start sentences, and special marks such as full stops, question marks and exclamation marks show where sentences end. The following sentence 'traffic jam' has no sentence boundaries. Can you read it?

itwasthefirstdayofspringthebirdsthathadbeen
quietthroughthelongwinterweresingingloudly
theytwitteredandcalledthroughtheforestwhat
awelcomesounditwaswhocouldbelievethatwint
erwasfinallyover

Here it is again, correctly punctuated.

> It was the first day of spring. The birds that had been quiet through the long winter were singing loudly. They twittered and called through the forest. What a welcome sound it was! Who could believe that winter was finally over?

In written English, punctuation marks are used to guide the reader and to make the writer's meaning clear. Punctuation marks:

✔ Act as sentence boundaries, showing where a sentence begins and where it ends. These punctuation marks are capital letters, full stops, question marks and exclamation marks.

✔ Are used within sentences. These punctuation marks include commas, colons, semicolons, ellipses, brackets, dashes and quotation marks.

✔ Are used within words. These punctuation marks include hyphens and apostrophes.

Conquering Commas

Commas break your sentences into chunks to help you communicate your exact meaning. The key is to put the commas where they help the reader to see and hear the sense of the sentence.

Using commas in lists

The shopping list says: torch batteries butter shortbread ice-cream cake. So how many things do you have to buy? Perhaps only three: torch batteries, butter shortbread, ice-cream cake. Or maybe six: torch, batteries, butter, shortbread, ice-cream, cake. No, it's four: torch batteries, butter shortbread, ice-cream, cake. How do you know? You don't, without the commas. So, here's what you need to buy, listed in a sentence:

> You need to buy torch batteries, butter shortbread, ice-cream and cake.

You need commas between the items in the list, with one important exception: you don't need one between the last two items. Why? Because the *and* is separating the last two items. But if you want to throw in an extra comma there, you can. It's not wrong. It's your choice.

The comma that comes before the *and* in a list of three or more items is so famous that it has its own name. It's called the *serial comma* or the *Oxford comma*. You don't need to remember what this list comma is called, but you do need to know how it can help you communicate more clearly.

Look at this sentence:

> Gemma did her school project about the explorers Leichhardt, Burke and Wills and Eyre.

If you didn't know that Burke and Wills belong together as a team, and Eyre worked solo, you might be confused. To be clear, this sentence needs the serial comma before the *and*:

> Gemma did her school project about the explorers Leichhardt, Burke and Wills, and Eyre.

To avoid confusion, in case the reader links the explorers into pairs, it's best to put the serial comma in this version too:

> Gemma did her school project about the explorers Burke and Wills, Leichhardt, and Eyre.

So the general rule here is this: if an item in the list already has an *and*, put a comma before the *and* between the last two items. You don't have to put a comma before the *and* in every list.

Punctuate the following sentence.

> Ando and Sully wrote their Christmas present list together and decided that they needed a skateboard a holiday in Noosa fish and chips a towel and a pair of boardies.

***Answer*:** Ando and Sully wrote their Christmas present list together and decided that they needed a skateboard, a holiday in Noosa, fish and chips, a towel and a pair of boardies. You can also put a comma after *towel* if you like.

Stringing adjectives together

To add personality and interest (and sometimes maybe even to stretch the truth), you enrich your sentences with *adjectives* and *adverbs*. (For more information on adjectives and adverbs, refer to Chapter 6.) Now look at the descriptions in the following sentence:

> When Mark dressed Ella in the outfit her grandparents had given her, she looked like a toddling frilly pink cushion.

No commas separate the three descriptive words in the sentence: *toddling*, *frilly* and *pink*. Using commas in lists of adjectives is not essential. It's a choice. So, the following tip sets out how to use them legally with adjectives if you choose to do so.

If you can put *and* between the adjectives comfortably, without disrupting the meaning of the description, it's okay to add a comma if you wish. So in the preceding example you'd get *a toddling* and *frilly* and *pink* cushion (which all sounds comfortable, so the commas are okay). But never put a comma between an adjective and the noun it's modifying.

Sometimes one descriptive word is clearly more important than the rest. All the descriptive words in a sentence may not deserve equal emphasis. Take a look at this example:

Lucinda just bought a funny, little, cocktail hat.

Here, you're giving equal weight to each of the three descriptions. Do you really want to do so? Probably not. Instead, you're likely to be emphasising that it's a *cocktail* hat. (Who buys cocktail hats these days?) So, you don't need to put commas between the other descriptions and would write it as 'a funny little cocktail hat'.

Using commas with determiners

Check out this sentence:

'I still have two big presents to save for,' said Maria.

No commas are used in *two big presents*. Would it be legal to write *two, big presents*? No. Why not? No comma appears after *two* because numbers are a different kind of modifier from descriptive adjectives. In grammar, numbers are *determiners*. They give you different information (how many presents or which presents, not what sort of presents). Try adding *and* between the words to hear this more clearly.

I've got two *and* big presents.

See, it doesn't work, does it?

Don't use commas to separate determiners from the words that they modify or from other descriptive words. (*Determiners* go in front of a noun and tell you how specific or otherwise something is — refer to Chapter 1 for more information.)

Addressing people directly

Traditionally, whenever you address someone directly, you need to separate the person's name from the rest of the sentence with a comma. Otherwise, your reader may misread the intention of the message. Take a look at the following:

> I gave the hinglefluber to your brother, Frank.

> I gave the hinglefluber to your brother Frank.

The first sentence is addressing Frank, and Frank has a brother who has the hinglefluber. In the second sentence, Frank has the hinglefluber.

In line with the trend to keep punctuation as uncomplicated as possible, this rule is being relaxed a little. So, in a short sentence, especially in informal communication like a note or a personal email, you can drop the comma. Like this:

> 'Thanks Frank.'

> 'Hi Clare.'

Noting introductory and concluding words

Sometimes, people set up what they're about to say with a word or two (as this sentence demonstrates). At other times, people tack some extra words on the end of a sentence. But how do you punctuate introductory or concluding elements? Read on.

Firstly, use a comma to separate introductory or concluding words from the rest of the sentence if the meaning of the sentence is not changed when you omit the extra element. Read these examples twice, once with the extra words and once without. See how the meaning stays the same?

> I don't like your attitude, no.

> Loud and over-confident, Jodie dominated the conversation.

Secondly, words that link a sentence to the idea that follows or precedes it are best set apart from the rest of the sentence with commas:

> For instance, Frank's hinglefluber could prove to be a useful deterrent.

> We may use it to keep Mildred's snake at bay, for example.

Thirdly, an element that modifies the whole sentence is separated from the rest of the sentence with a comma. Like these:

Unfortunately, your garment was eaten by the tumble dryer.

Your white shorts are now pink, apparently.

If, however, your sentence contains an element that can't be removed without changing the meaning of the sentence, the comma is optional. You can choose whether or not to use it.

Yesterday the rules seemed so much clearer.

Yesterday, the rules seemed so much clearer.

The rules seemed so much clearer yesterday.

In some situations, however, leaving the comma out can confuse the reader. Consider this sentence:

After winning his head grew even fatter.

Did you read *After winning his head* as the introductory element? Adding the comma leaves no room for confusion. The reader pauses at the comma and the meaning is clear:

After winning, his head grew even fatter.

To sum up, use a comma to separate an introductory or concluding element from the rest of the sentence if that element can be removed from the sentence without changing the meaning, if it connects ideas, or if it modifies the whole sentence. Otherwise, you can leave it out unless its omission creates confusion for the reader.

Adding extra detail with pairs of commas

When you add information that's not strictly necessary into a sentence, you need a pair of commas to mark off that extra information from the rest of the sentence. This includes descriptions and further explanations, as well as words that are interruptions to the main sentence — words such as *therefore*, *of course* and *by the way*. Consider the following sentences with and without commas:

Politicians, who gather information from social media, are not to be trusted.

Politicians who gather information from social media are not to be trusted.

What's the difference? In sentence one, *who gather information from social media* is a description of *politicians*. It's extra information. So, it's set off from the rest of the sentence by commas. You can take it out and the sentence still means the same thing — *Politicians are not to be trusted.* None of them. Not ever. And, by the way, they all use social media as a source of information. But do not trust them.

Without the commas, as in the second example, the information becomes essential to the meaning of the sentence. It can't be removed without altering what you're saying. Without commas, the description changes the subject of the sentence from the noun *Politicians* to the noun group *Politicians who use social media*. It gives the reader essential information about the meaning of *politicians* in this sentence. This sentence is warning that you can trust some politicians but not others. Do not trust the ones who gather information from social media.

Remember that commas travel in pairs as far as extra information is concerned. Don't use just one comma where you need two. When reading over what you've written, stop at the commas to check whether the information that follows can be removed from a sentence. If it can, put another comma at the end of the information.

Never put a comma between a subject and its verb, even if the subject is really long. Look at this sentence:

> RIGHT: The guy who I met last night at the tram stop carries a purple man-bag.

> WRONG: The guy, who I met last night at the tram stop, carries a purple man-bag.

The first sentence is correct because the subject that matches the main verb of the sentence (*carries*) is *The guy who I met last night at the tram stop*. The second sentence is wrong because, if you take out the information between the commas, the sentence doesn't easily make sense. It becomes *The guy carries a purple man-bag.* What guy? The complete subject no longer comes before the verb.

Connecting commas with conjunctions

When you join two complete sentences with the conjunctions *and, or, but, nor, yet* or *so*, it can help your readers if you put a comma before the conjunction. However, it is not essential and the comma is usually omitted if the sentences being joined are short. Here are some examples:

> Mike may tell Susie when they have dinner together next week, or he may tell her today.

> Mike may tell her tonight or he may remain silent.

The rule of never putting a comma between a subject and its verb also applies with sentences that have one subject (who or what you're talking about) and two verbs joined by *and, or, but, nor, yet* or *so*. Don't put commas between the two verbs. You aren't joining two complete sentences, just two words or groups of words. Here are two examples:

> WRONG: Susie said nothing, but stared very loudly.

> WHY IT'S WRONG: The sentence has one subject (*Susie*) that has two verbs (*said* and *stared*). You aren't joining two complete sentences here, so you shouldn't place a comma before the conjunction (*but*).

> RIGHT: When Mike told Susie, Susie said nothing but stared very loudly.

Simplifying Semicolons

Think of the highest selling series of books for the past century. No, nothing to do with the colour grey! Remember that boy wizard? *Harry Potter* reaches readers aged 8 to 80, and these novels are littered with colons and semicolons. Truly. You don't need to be a wizard to use them correctly.

Hinging complete thoughts

A semicolon (;) can join one complete sentence to another. It's a stronger piece of punctuation than a comma, but not as strong as a full stop. Think of a semicolon as a hinge connecting two sentences. An example:

> Stevo broke a bootlace; he went to the shop.

You can't just join any two sentences in this way. The sentences that semicolons join must relate logically to each other. (You wouldn't hinge the door to the window frame!) Look at this sample:

> Stevo broke a bootlace; he loves his job.

It's hard to see the connection between these ideas. The two ideas would be better expressed in separate sentences.

Joining with conjuncts

Conjuncts are transition words that help create a logical connection between ideas. The most common conjuncts are *however, consequently, also, moreover, therefore, nevertheless, besides, thus, indeed, still, otherwise, similarly, for example* and *for instance*. Conjuncts provide links, but they're not real conjunctions. So, you need to understand how they co-exist with semicolons. For instance:

> When the Lonely Hearts Club caught fire, Mr Kite ushered everyone outside; however, Maxwell rushed into the burning building to rescue his silver hammer.

Or this:

> When the Lonely Hearts Club caught fire, Mr Kite ushered everyone outside. Maxwell, however, rushed into the burning building to rescue his silver hammer.

In the first sample, two complete sentences are connected by *however*. So, it has a semicolon before it and a comma after it. In the second sample, the *however* is perfectly correct with a comma on either side of it because it isn't trying to join two sentences together.

Correct or incorrect?

A. Yoko sang with all her heart; therefore, the glass in the recording booth shattered.

B. Yoko sang with all her heart, therefore, the glass in the recording booth shattered.

C. Yoko sang with all her heart. Therefore, the glass in the recording booth shattered.

Answer: Sentences A and C are correct, but sentence B is incorrect. *Therefore* is a false joiner. If you want to use it, add a semicolon or start a new sentence.

Here's the bottom line: in combining two complete sentences, be sure to use at least a semicolon or a conjunction. They have muscles. Don't use a comma or a conjunct (a false joiner). They're not strong enough.

Separating items in a list with semicolons

Red Belly is writing his guest list for his annual Australia Day barbeque. He plans to invite quite a few important people. Here, without punctuation, are some of the lucky guests:

> Digger Dugite the nation's leading reptile historian Francine Frill the dragon expert a keeper from the local zoo the movie villain known as Copperhead and of course William Worm-skink his local member of parliament.

Confusing, isn't it? Perhaps commas will help:

> Digger Dugite, the nation's leading reptile historian, Francine Frill, the dragon expert, a keeper from the local zoo, the movie villain known as Copperhead, and, of course, William Worm-skink, his local member of parliament.

The caterer wants to know how many people to cook for, but the list has some names, some titles and some descriptions. Which of the names, titles and descriptions are paired, indicating one person? Are eight people invited or only five? How can you tell?

If the list isn't punctuated or is punctuated only with commas, you can't tell the difference. All those names and titles are jumbled together. You need something stronger than a comma to separate the elements of the list. You need — super comma! Well, actually you need semicolons. Here's the correct version:

> Red Belly is writing his guest list for his annual Australia Day barbeque. He plans to invite Digger Dugite, the nation's leading reptile historian; Francine Frill, the dragon expert; a keeper from the local zoo; the movie villain known as Copperhead; and, of course, William Worm-skink, his local member of parliament.

The rule for semicolons in lists is very simple:

- ✔ When any items in a list include commas, separate all the items with semicolons.

- ✔ Put a semicolon between the last two items on the list (before the conjunction). Note that a comma here is optional if you separate items with commas (refer to the section 'Using commas in lists', earlier in this chapter, for more information). But you must use a semicolon between the last two items if you're using semicolons for your list (leaving it out isn't an option).

Which is correct?

A. While she watched the football match with Cathy, Deborah thought of all the things she had to do: wash up the dishes, which had been piling up since last time she visited, sell the house, decide how to talk Noel into letting her keep the dog, which she was very fond of, and arrange a day at the spa to cheer herself up.

B. While she watched the football match with Cathy, Deborah thought of all the things she had to do: wash up the dishes, which had been piling up since last time she visited; sell the house; decide how to talk Noel into letting her keep the dog, which she was very fond of; and arrange a day at the spa to cheer herself up.

Answer: The punctuation of sentence B is correct. Two of the items in the list have commas in them:

wash up the dishes, which had been piling up since last time she visited

decide how to talk Noel into letting her keep the dog, which she was very fond of

So you must separate the items on the list with semicolons. Remember that you need a semicolon before the word *and*.

Clarifying Colons

Here is the most frequent use of colons these days — gasp! :-0 open mouth of shock. Traditionally, though, a colon (:) like its younger sibling the semicolon, shows up when a simple comma isn't strong enough to connect ideas. A colon draws attention to the material that follows it. It is used to introduce information that develops or explains the words preceding the colon.

Setting up long lists

The colon precedes the first item of a lengthy list. Like this:

Lucinda's list of things to do in her life included the following: work for a major fashion designer, buy a small island, have a big white wedding, star in a reality series and see all her diamonds being cut.

The words before the colon should form a complete thought. If you put a colon in front of a list, check the beginning of the sentence to be sure it makes complete sense on its own.

Setting up extracts

Use a colon before a long extract or quotation taken from somewhere else. Such extracts are called *block quotes*. So here's how you'd punctuate a review of Tiffany's new novel:

> I found some of the writing to be so sugary sweet that I feared it would give me cavities. Passages like this made me want to suck a lemon:
>
> > Candy was looking forward to another wonderful day in Treacle Town. The new job excited her so. The warmth of her new colleagues made her smile on the inside even bigger than the gorgeous glowing grin she showed the world.

Notice, too, that the block quote is set-in (indented). Throughout this book we use a colon when we introduce sample sentences and examples. They're being treated like block quotes.

Expanding on an idea

In one special situation, colons show up inside sentences, joining one complete sentence to another or perhaps to a sentence fragment (a piece of a sentence). When the second idea explains, restates or summarises the meaning of the first idea, you may join the ideas with a colon. And you can do this whether the information following the colon is a complete sentence or just a sentence fragment. Like this:

> Jude has a problem: he doesn't know how to improve his sad song. (two sentences)

> Jude sings only one kind of song: sad. (sentence + fragment)

For the want of a colon

Have you ever giggled at ambiguous signs like these:

Cattle in Paddocks Please Close the Gate

Native Flora Stay on Pathways

They conjure up amusing mental images: a huge black Angus balanced precariously on hind legs while trying to manipulate the gate latch with bovine hooves, or a huddle of wayward gum trees and wattles bumping into each other in an attempt to stay on the path. However, with just a little bit of editing and some working knowledge of the rules for placing colons, these signs could communicate in a clear, unambiguous way.

The first thing you'd need to do is apply the rule about putting a complete sentence at the start of the communication. In each of the sample signs, this could easily be achieved by reversing the order of the information, because in each case, a complete *imperative sentence* is used. The word *imperative* means necessary or crucial. So an *imperative sentence* gives a command or instruction:

Please Close the Gate

Stay on Pathways

Now that you have the first part of the communication complete, what you need to do next is add your friend the trusty colon. Then, you can follow that up with the information that explains why following the command is imperative:

Please Close the Gate: Cattle in Paddock

Stay on Pathways: Native Flora

See? Ambiguity gone. The changes may require an additional two dots of paint, but the resulting signs communicate far more efficiently.

Dealing with Dashes

You may not even realise that punctuation aficionados enjoy using dashes of three different lengths (although one is called a hyphen and not a dash). Read on and be amazed.

Using the humble hyphen with words

A *hyphen* is a short dash used to link two words or word parts so that they do the work of one word. Hyphens are used to form compound words such as *brother-in-law*, *ex-wife*, *pro-choice*, *one-way*, *passer-by* and *home-cooked*. Hyphens can also make the meaning of a word clear. For example, re-creation means 'to create again', whereas recreation means 'leisure'. Don't put a space before or after the hyphen.

Here's a simple rule concerning hyphens: If two words are being used as a single description, put a hyphen between them if the description comes before the word that it's describing. That is, if the words are being used as an adjective. For example:

> We need a long-term solution.

but

> We can't go on doing this in the long term. (Because *long term* isn't describing anything here, it's a noun, not an adjective.)

The issue is ambiguity. If we had written *long term solution*, you may be confused about whether the solution is *long-term* or is it a long *term-solution*? The hyphen makes the meaning clear: *long* is describing *term*. You don't need to hyphenate two-word descriptions if the first word is an adverb (most of these end in *-ly*), because rarely any ambiguity exists:

> fully understood idea
>
> completely ridiculous grammar rule

You can't have a *fully idea* or a *completely rule* so it's obvious what the meaning is.

Well also causes problems sometimes. Follow the same rule here. Use a hyphen if it's part of a word that comes before the word it's qualifying, and leave the hyphen out otherwise. So:

> I like a well-placed hyphen.
>
> That hyphen is well placed.

You can use a hyphen to create exactly the right combination of words to express your thought. You might want to create a *never-before-seen* adjective to describe that *hard-to-explain* thing. You can do it with *annoying-but-ever-so-useful* hyphens!

Sometimes it's difficult to know whether a compound is two separate words, two words connected with a hyphen, or just one word — *car park*, *car-park* or *carpark*. Often this is the process that words go through when they change. If you don't know whether a particular expression needs a hyphen, check a current Australian dictionary.

Place hyphens where they're needed in this paragraph:

> Vicky was recently elected secretary treasurer of her local reading group. Over two thirds of the members voted for her. Some of them think that she can get Edgar to speak to the group, but she also has many kind hearted friends.

Answer: Here's the paragraph with the hyphens inserted, along with explanations in parentheses:

> Vicky was recently elected secretary-treasurer (a hyphen is needed for a compound title) of her local reading group. Over two-thirds of the members (a hyphen is needed for this fraction) voted for her. Some of them think that she can get Edgar to speak to the group, but she also has many kind-hearted friends (add a hyphen to a two-word adjective or check a dictionary to see if it's made it to one-word status).

Using the humble hyphen with numbers

Another common use of hyphens is with numbers:

- ✔ Hyphenate all the numbers from twenty-one to ninety-nine.

- ✔ Hyphenate all fractions used as descriptions (*three-quarters full, nine-tenths finished*).

- ✔ Don't hyphenate fractions preceded by *a* or *an* (*a half of his brain, an eighth of an octopus*).

- ✔ Use hyphens where numbers and words are combined into an adjective (*19-year-old genius, ten-year-old wine, two-part series, three-ring circus*).

Use hyphens when you talk about someone who is *a 12-year-old* or *an 80-year-old*. Why? Because the term is still being treated as an adjective or determiner, even though a noun doesn't follow it. You're talking about *a 12-year-old child* or *an 80-year-old person*. Even though the last word (the noun) isn't said, it is understood. Don't use a hyphen, however, if you're using just the number as a determiner: *12 years old, 80 years young*.

Embracing em and en dashes

Dashes can look like this (—) or like this (–). The long dash is called an *em rule* or *em dash*. (*Rule* is just printer- and editor-speak for *line*.) The short one is called an *en rule* or *en dash*. They're so named because originally the em rule was as wide as a capital M and the en rule was as wide as an N. Each one of these dashes has a particular use.

An em rule can be set with or without a space on each side. It's a style choice. You'll notice that in this book we use the spaced em dash — an elegant, easy-to-read choice!

Dashes are used to indicate extra information. Unlike brackets (see the following section), they do not always have to be in pairs. For example, the following is a perfectly legal (and very pleasant) sentence:

> It was a classic beach day — hot sun, perfect surf and a slight breeze.

A pair of dashes can also be used to show a strong interruption from the rest of the sentence:

> My favourite day of the year — apart from my birthday, I suppose — is Christmas Day.

Em dashes tell the reader that you've jumped tracks onto a new subject for a moment. They can add extra information in the middle of a sentence (in which case you need a pair of dashes, just as you would need a pair of brackets or commas) or they can add something on the end (in which case, you need only one dash). Here are some more examples:

> After we take the dogs for a good long run — I forgot to tell you about my greyhounds — we'll stop at the pub.

> Vicky was nearly killed when crossing the road last night — by a pair of speeding greyhounds.

Which of these are correct?

A. Everyone who saw the accident — even Dr Jones, who's a devoted dog-lover himself, agreed that Vicky was not at fault.

B. Everyone who saw the accident — even Dr Jones, who's a devoted dog-lover — agreed that Vicky was not at fault.

C. Everyone who saw the accident agreed that Vicky was not at fault — even Dr Jones, who's a devoted dog-lover.

D. Everyone who saw the accident (even Dr Jones, who's a devoted dog-lover) agreed that Vicky was not at fault.

Answer: Sentence A is wrong. If you stop the sentence at the dash, you lose the end of the sentence. *Everyone who saw the accident* on its own isn't complete. Sentence B is correct, where we've brought the end of the sentence back (*agreed that Vicky was not at fault*) after the second dash. So are sentence C, where we've reassembled the main idea of the sentence before the dash, and sentence D, where we've used brackets instead (see following section).

An en dash is pretty technical. It has three main uses:

- To link spans, such as numbers in addresses, distances or times (*12–14 Station Street, aged 8–10, June–July, Sydney–Hobart yacht race*)

- To connect words that have a clear association, but where each retains its exact meaning and separate identity when joined (*hand–eye coordination, the Asia–Pacific region, Queensland–Northern Territory border*)

- To join names to indicate that you're talking about more than one person (*Costanza–Seinfeld effect, Cooper–Hoffstader theory*).

Dashes should be used sparingly. Your writing containing a lot of dashes is often a sign that your sentences are too long for readers to understand easily. Edit!

Bracketing Information

Brackets (or parentheses) enclose extra information, such as an example, comment or explanation. They are used to separate the information inside them from the rest of the sentence and are always used in pairs:

Sophie Moylan (who you met last week) was there.

Brackets are also called *parentheses* and come in several different shapes. *Round brackets* ( ) surround words that provide extra (not essential) information about the main idea of the sentence. They can also surround the numbers or letters of a list and surround the source of something quoted. *Square brackets* [ ] are used to add to, explain or change someone else's words within a quotation. *Angle brackets* < > are often used around web addresses.

Sometimes, putting words inside round brackets is useful. Doing so separates those words from the rest of the sentence to give them a specific emphasis. Because brackets come in pairs, it's a good idea to check what you've written to make sure both halves of the pair are there when you use brackets. (If you need to put brackets inside brackets, use square brackets [also just called *brackets*] for the inside pair.) Just like the preceding sentence.

The rules for adding a full stop with brackets (round or square) are clear. A full stop belongs to the sentence, not to the words in brackets. The full stop only goes inside the brackets if the whole sentence is inside the brackets. Look at this example:

WRONG: Susie loves Christmas, especially now that Max is old enough to enjoy it. (She particularly misses her mother at Christmas, though).

RIGHT: Susie loves Christmas, especially now that Max is old enough to enjoy it. (She particularly misses her mother at Christmas, though.)

And one more rule: you should never put a comma *before* an opening bracket. Look at this sentence:

WRONG: All year round, but especially in the summer, (when the nights are hot), Raj suffers from insomnia.

ALSO WRONG: All year round, but especially in the summer, (when the nights are hot) Raj suffers from insomnia.

RIGHT: All year round, but especially in the summer (when the nights are hot), Raj suffers from insomnia.

EVEN BETTER: All year round, but especially in the summer when the nights are hot, Raj suffers from insomnia. (Don't overuse brackets.)

See Chapter 10 for more information on using brackets when using quotation marks.

Chapter 8

Apostrophes: They're There for a Reason

The world is full of advertising. Daily, you're likely to see countless businesses promoting themselves and retailers trying to lure you to purchase their wares with signs displaying apostrophe catastrophes like these:

Fresh tomato's

Smiths Furniture — the Best Deal's in Town!

Apostrophes are those little tadpoles like high-flying commas that hang around close to the tops of letters. They're also the most misused and abused of all punctuation marks — a fact that irritates many self-confessed lovers of correctness. They would correct the signs in our sample to read:

Fresh tomatoes

Smith's Furniture — the Best Deals in Town!

Even very well educated people throw in those little taddies where they don't belong and leave them out where they're needed. In this chapter, we explain how to shorten words with apostrophes, how to use apostrophes to show ownership and how to form some plurals.

Shortening Words with Contractions

A *contraction* shortens a word by removing one letter or more and substituting an apostrophe in the same spot. For example, chop *wi* out of *I will*, throw in an apostrophe, and you have *I'll*. The resulting word is shorter and faster to say.

Take a look at Table 8-1 for a list of common contractions. Note that some are irregular. (*Won't*, for example, is short for *will* not.)

Table 8-1		Contractions	
Phrase	*Contraction*	*Phrase*	*Contraction*
are not	aren't	she would	she'd
cannot	can't	that is	that's
could not	couldn't	they are	they're
did not	didn't	they will	they'll
do not	don't	they would	they'd
does not	doesn't	we are	we're
he had	he'd	we had	we'd
he is	he's	we have	we've
he will	he'll	we will or we shall	we'll
he would	he'd	we would	we'd
I am	I'm	what has	what's
I had	I'd	what is	what's
I have	I've	who has	who's
I will or I shall	I'll	who is	who's
I would	I'd	will not	won't
is not	isn't	would not	wouldn't

Using Apostrophes to Show Possession

English gives you two ways of indicating ownership or possession: With or without an apostrophe. For example:

the house of my friend = my friend's house

the letters of the lovers = the lovers' letters

the fine milkshakes of that corner cafe = that corner cafe's fine milkshakes

 To use the possessive apostrophe correctly (to mean 'belonging to'), first decide whether the noun is singular (one) or plural (more than one), and then add the apostrophe. Doing so helps to ensure that the *s* and the apostrophe are in the correct order — *friend's house* is singular. *Lovers' letters* is plural.

Showing ownership with singular nouns

To show possession by one owner, here's the rule: First add an apostrophe and then the letter *s* to the owner. Examples are:

The *dragon's* claws (The claws belong to the dragon.)

Captain Cavity's gold-filled tooth (The gold-filled tooth belongs to Captain Cavity.)

 Another way to think about this rule is to see whether the word *of* expresses what you're trying to say. Check these examples:

the cover *of* the atlas = the *atlas's* cover

the long memory *of* the elephant = the *elephant's* long memory

Showing ownership with plural nouns

The plurals of most English nouns — anything greater than one — already end in *s*. To show ownership, all you do is add an apostrophe after the *s*. Take a look at these examples:

four *dogs'* muddy paws (That's 16 muddy paws belonging to four dogs.)

the *dinosaurs'* petrified eggs (The petrified eggs belong to the dinosaurs.)

the 12 *roses'* fading petals (The fading petals belong to the 12 roses.)

In Australia, we don't use apostrophes in place or street names. So you'll find names like *Flinders Street*, *Kings Cross*, *St Patricks Place* and *Berrys Beach*.

Companies, shops and other organisations also own things, so these proper nouns (nouns that begin with a capital letter) also get apostrophes. Put the apostrophe at the end of the name. For example:

> *Heinz's* 57 varieties
>
> *RM Williams'* boots

You can sometimes avoid the whole problem of the apostrophe by thinking of the owner as a sort of adjective instead: *Heinz varieties, RM Williams boots, Telstra profits.* This doesn't always work, but it can get you out of some tricky situations.

Which is correct?

A. Dr Mackenzie was worried about her son's behaviour.

B. Dr Mackenzie was worried about her sons' behaviour.

Answer: Sentence A is correct if you're talking about one son. Sentence B is correct if you're talking about more than one.

Irregular plural possessives

Of course, not all plural English words end in *s*. Lots of them are irregular. To show ownership for an irregular plural (one that doesn't end in *s*), add an apostrophe and then the letter *s*. Like this:

> the *children's* pet mice (The mice belong to the children.)
>
> the *mice's* feet (The feet belong to the mice.)

Compound plural possessives

An apostrophe can apply to a whole group of words (not just the one it's connected to). For example:

> *Keith, Nicole, Sunday Rose and Faith's* house (The house is home to all of them.)

However, if two people own things separately, as individuals, you should use two apostrophes to make this clearer:

> Her *sister's* and *Jacque's* cars were parked outside. (Two people, two cars.)

Collective noun possessives

Some nouns are used to indicate a collection or group, like *team*, *herd* and *army*. *Collective nouns* stand for more than one object, but you should treat the group as one thing. So:

> The *team's* defeat
>
> The *school's* reputation.

Remember that an apostrophe shows ownership. Don't use an apostrophe when you have just a simple plural (a word that's *not* expressing ownership). Here are some examples:

> RIGHT: Tomatoes aren't to everyone's taste.
>
> WRONG: Tomatoe's aren't to everyone's taste.

Place apostrophes where they're needed in this paragraph:

> Bills offer to go to Bettys to collect the cake for George and Vickys party was gratefully accepted. He had to go shopping anyway because he needed food for the puppies dinner and a card for his brothers birthday. Jane would have gone, but she had a lot to do to prepare for her parents party. She wasn't sure if candles were required for an anniversary cake, so she asked Bill to get some and made a note to ask her friends what they thought.

Answer: Bill's offer to go to Betty's to collect the cake for George and Vicky's party was gratefully accepted. He had to go shopping anyway because he needed food for the puppies' dinner and a card for his brother's birthday. Jane would have gone, but she had a lot to do to prepare for her parents' party. She wasn't sure if candles were required for an anniversary cake, so she asked Bill to get some and made a note to ask her friends what they thought.

Possessives with hyphens

For words with *hyphens* — son-in-law, mother-of-pearl, 20-year-old — the rule is simple: put the apostrophe at the end of the word, never inside it. For example:

> the *dogcatcher-in-chief's* canine teeth (The canine teeth belong to the dogcatcher-in-chief.)
>
> the *doctors-of-philosophy's* common room (The room is for the use of all the doctors-of-philosophy.)

Possessives ending in s

Singular nouns that end in *s* present special problems. Jimmy Barnes has recorded a lot of songs, but the name *Barnes* is singular, because he is only one person. Hence:

> I love Jimmy *Barnes'* raspy style.

or

> Jimmy *Barnes's* screaming is not singing.

Both of these sentences are grammatically correct (whether or not you agree with the opinions they express). Why? Firstly, it has to do with sound. If the letter *s* crops up too many times, the words can be hard to say (and you can find yourself hissing and spitting all over your listener). Secondly, some grammarians assert that if a name has only one syllable and ends with *s*, you should add only an apostrophe.

Others, like us, prefer to go with the KISS principle rather than complicate the issue. We're big fans of an 'always rule'. So if you always add an apostrophe plus another *s* to a singular name, whatever letter it ends with, you'll always be right.

Apostrophes with possessive pronouns

English also supplies pronouns — words that take the place of a noun — for ownership. Here are some possessive pronouns: *mine*, *yours*, *his*, *hers*, *its*, *ours* and *theirs*. None of these possessive pronouns ever has an apostrophe.

> WRONG: Each dog has it's own favourite chair.

> RIGHT: Each dog has its own favourite chair.

Which sentence is correct?

A. Jessica's parents are telling everyone that Hugh is a friend of their's.

B. Jessica's parents are telling everyone that Hugh is a friend of theirs.

C. Jessicas parents are telling everyone that Hugh is a friend of theirs.

Answer: Sentence B is correct. In sentence A, the apostrophe is needed in *Jessica's* because the parents belong to Jessica. However, *their's* should not have an apostrophe because no possessive pronoun ever has an apostrophe. In sentence C, *theirs* is written correctly, but *Jessicas* needs an apostrophe.

For more information on possessive pronouns, refer to Chapter 5.

TIP

Who's whose

Whose shows ownership. It seldom causes any problems, except when it's confused with another word: *who's*. *Who's* is a contraction that's short for *who is*.

In other words:

Sandy, *whose* cooking leaves a lot to be desired, wonders *who's* going to accept her dinner invitation.

and

Whose bar of chocolate is on the radiator? *Who's* stupid enough to put chocolate on a radiator?

Here are more correct examples for your consideration:

Whose review will Shannon read first?

Who's going to tell John that his eyebrows have knots in them?

Using Apostrophes with Abbreviations and Numbers

The rules for abbreviations and numbers are exactly the same as the rules for words. An apostrophe indicates possession:

The R&R's effect on her was instant.

I think 1963's hits have always been my favourites.

To make an abbreviation or a number into a plural, just add a lower-case *s*. Don't use a capital *s* or add an apostrophe:

Shane was dismayed when the new PCs arrived.

Mia thinks photographs of her parents in the 1960s are hilarious.

An exception to this rule (of course, an exception has to exist!) occurs if you need to refer to letters of the alphabet:

Harley's g's look just like his q's.

Think of a word with three i's.

Chapter 9

Choosing Capital Letters and Numerals

In This Chapter

▶ Understanding when capitals are required (and when they're not)

▶ Choosing between numerals and words

*W*hen you write a text to a mate, you probably don't bother to use capital letters, and when you're busy at the keyboard, your word processor probably pops a few in for you as you type. But what do you do when you're writing an essay or preparing your CV for your first part-time job application? Well, naturally, you flip open this trusty little reference book at the appropriate page and follow our advice. In this chapter, we cover a few of the stickier points of capitalisation to help you impress with accuracy. We also give you some pointers on numbers — in particular, how to decide whether to use numerals or words.

Covering the Basics of Capitalisation

Fortunately, the basic rules for capital letters are easy:

✔ Begin every sentence with a capital letter.

✔ Capitalise the pronoun *I*.

✔ Begin quotations with a capital letter unless you're jumping to the middle of a quotation.

Don't change anything to a capital that's been deliberately named with a lower case letter, though. For example, internet addresses are almost always in lower case, you'll find poems attributed to an American poet known as e. e. cummings, some brand names reject capital letters and Daniel Johns and friends named their band silverchair.

Speaking officially

Meet *Mr* George Robinson, a *director* of a small local printing firm. George has aspirations to be *Lord Mayor of Sydney*. Mind you, next year, the *Archbishop of Sydney* also plans to run for the local council. His sister is pleased that George may be a *councillor*, but hopes he'll never be *Governor General*. Now what's going on with the capitals? Here are some general rules:

- ✔ Abbreviated titles (*Mr*, *Mrs*, *Miss* and *Ms*, but also *Dr*, *Prof.*, *Rev.* and so on) are always capitalised because they're attached to names. (If they are used alone, they're usually written out as, for example, *mister* and *missus*.)

- ✔ Titles like *director* and *councillor*, which refer to lots of people (more than one director exists and more than one councillor), are capitalised if associated with a name but not if on their own. (So you'd write *Lieutenant Jones*, but he's been promoted to the rank of *lieutenant*.)

- ✔ Titles that belong to only one person at a time (for example, the Secretary-General of the United Nations, the President of the United States, the Prime Minister of Australia and the Premier of Queensland) are capitalised when you're referring to one particular holder of the title. They're not given capitals when you're referring to the positions in a general way. (So you'd write to the Minister for Planning to complain that other *ministers* are contradicting what he's said.)

Addressing family

The rule for capitalising the titles of family members is simple. If the title takes the place of a name (as in *Grandma* instead of *Gladys*), capitalise it.

> Bill's brother Mike took their cousin's son to the zoo. (*Brother* and *cousin* are general kinship labels, not names, in this sentence.)

> He was embarrassed when Grandma Robinson saw him waddling past the penguin pool. (*Grandma Robinson* is a specific name.)

Try substituting a real name for the family label in your sentence. If it fits, you need a capital letter. Let's substitute the name *Zeke* for the kinship label *dad* to see how this works:

> RIGHT: I told my *dad* that I was leaving.

> WEIRD: I told my *Zeke* that I was leaving.

> WRONG: I told my *Dad* that I was leaving.

See? So you don't need the capital letter in the sample sentence because *dad* cannot be replaced by his name.

Which sentence is correct?

A. 'Tell mum I won't be home for dinner tonight,' said Rashid.

B. 'Tell Mum I won't be home for dinner tonight,' said Rashid.

Answer: Sentence B is correct. *Mum* is used as a name, so you must capitalise it. (The test works!)

Capitalising directions

Deciding whether to use a capital letter for the names of the points of a compass can cause confusion. A rough guide is that if you're talking about a specific part of the world, capitalise the words *North, South, East* and *West* but use lower case if you're just talking about a direction.

Another general rule is that, if one of these words is used as an adjective, sometimes the phrase becomes recognised as a geographical entity (South Korea, West Africa or the North Shore, for example) and then the adjective is capitalised. Otherwise, it isn't (eastern Sydney, northern Australia).

The names of other, smaller areas are often capitalised too. Melbourne (and Brisbane) has a South Bank. New York has a West Side. London has an East End. These have capital letters because they're the names of specific parts of the city.

Understanding geographical capital letters

Generally, the names of countries and cities, the languages spoken there, and the nationalities and ethnicities of the people who live there take capital letters. So you're pretty safe if you use a capital for any word that expresses direct connection with a place.

You should also capitalise locations within a country when the proper name is given (the name of a suburb or region, for example). Be sure to capitalise the entire name. Here are some examples:

- ✔ the Bungle Bungles
- ✔ Pakenham Upper
- ✔ the Murray River

When the name doesn't appear, use lower case for geographical features such as *mountain*, *valley*, *gorge* and *beach*.

Is *the* part of a geographical name? Usually not, even when it's hard to imagine the name without it. In general, don't capitalise *the*.

A few countries have kindly lent their names to common objects: *French fries*, *Scotch whisky*, *Dutch oven*. Most people (and dictionaries) capitalise these. Some of these terms, however, have become so commonly used that they no longer refer to things with a direct connection to that place. So, their capital letter has been lost: *roman type*, *venetian blinds*. You need to check your trusty, up-to-date, Australian dictionary to be sure which ones need capitals.

You need to be extra careful when discussing race and ethnicity. Black and White (or black and white) are acceptable, but be consistent. Don't capitalise one and not the other. It's best to refer to Indigenous Australians, sometimes also called Australian Aborigines, as Aboriginal and Torres Strait Islander peoples. Some people make the mistake of thinking Koori/Koorie has the same meaning as Aboriginal (*Koori* is a broad term for Aboriginal people of New South Wales and Victoria).

Talking about history

If you had a time machine, where would you go? Would you set the dial for the *Bronze Age*, *Middle Ages* or the middle of the *Dreamtime*? You should probably select a *period* that didn't involve a *war*: the *Second World War* may be interesting to historians, but it wasn't much fun to live through. How about the *19th century*? Or the *Depression*? Perhaps you're really only interested in the *Eureka Stockade*.

The preceding paragraph should make the rules concerning the capitalisation of historical events and eras easy. Capitalise the names of specific time periods and events but not general words. Hence:

- ✓ Capitalised: Bronze Age, Dreaming, Second World War, Depression, Eureka Stockade
- ✓ Lower case: period, war

Everyone capitalises the Second World War, but some people call it World War II or WW2. Be consistent: Don't mix and match.

Correct the capitalisation in this paragraph.

Mozart once met Marie Antoinette, but it was before Bastille Day and the French revolution, when she was a child. The 18th Century must have seemed to her to be a good time to be alive.

Answer: The explanations are in parentheses.

Mozart once met Marie Antoinette, but it was before Bastille Day (correct: capitalise the names of important days) and the French Revolution (the revolution was a unique event and should, therefore, be capitalised — you capitalise names of wars), when she was a child. The 18th century (a style choice, but we prefer to lower-case numbered centuries) must have seemed to her to be a good time to be alive.

Referring to times and times of year

After reading the following example, you can probably figure out the rule for using capitals with seasons and times without help:

Lochness hates the *summer* because of all the tourists who try to snap pictures of 'an imaginary monster'. She's been known to roar something about '*winter's* peaceful *mornings*', even though she never wakes up before *1 pm*. Lochie especially loves *the winter solstice* and *leap years*.

Write the seasons of the year in lower case, as well as the times of day. Poetry is an exception, but everyone knows that poets make up their own rules, so those exceptions don't count.

When writing times, the abbreviation *am* stands for *ante meridian*, when the sun hasn't yet reached its highest point (the *meridian*). *Ante* is Latin for *before*. The other term — *pm* — stands for *post meridian*, when the sun has passed its highest point in the sky. *Post* is Latin for *after*.

Some people like to separate these time abbreviations with full stops, but Australian style is to leave out the full stops. Put a space between the number and the abbreviation. So you should write:

8.00 am, 9.52 pm, 11 am

Looking at titles

Bella is planning a party to celebrate the release of Stephanie's latest novel, *INDIGO DUSK: A TALE OF LOVE AND WEREWOLVES* (at least that's the way its name looks in the design on the cover). She is procrastinating about sending the invitations because she can't decide how to capitalise the title. What should she do? Well, that depends whether she wants to go for minimal capital letters, in which case she'd only use capitals for the first word and any proper nouns in the title. (Notice also that titles are written in italics.) So it'd be:

> *Indigo dusk: a tale of love and werewolves*

Or, if she wanted to go for maximum effect with maximal capital letters, she would use a capital letter for the first word of the title, the first word of the subtitle, plus any other word that's not an article, preposition or coordinating conjunction. (Refer to Chapter 4 for more on prepositions.) So she would write:

> *Indigo Dusk: A Tale of Love and Werewolves*

Whichever style she chooses, it's important that she's consistent.

When writing the title of a magazine or newspaper, should you capitalise and italicise the word *the*? The answer used to be: 'Yes', if *the* is part of the official name, as in *The Age*; 'No', if the publication didn't include *the* in its official name, as in the *Mercury*. Now, however, it's increasingly more common in Australia not to bother at all.

Official Australian style suggests that you should use *The* with the title if it doesn't overlap with use of the ordinary word *the* in your sentence. Here's how it works:

> Julia read something surprising in the editorial of *The Canberra Times*.

> Julia read something surprising in the *Canberra Times* editorial.

In the first sentence, *The Canberra Times* is given as the name of the paper containing the editorial, and you don't need another *the* in front of it. While in the second sentence, what we mean is 'in the *The Canberra Times* editorial'. Only we're not actually saying that in as many words, because it would be silly to have *the The*. So, we drop *The* from the title of the newspaper and just use the ordinary definite article *the* in our sentence. Get it?

Descriptions of eras are sometimes shortened to capital letters such as *BP* (*before present*), *CE* (*of the common era*), *BC* (*before Christ*) and *AD* (*anno Domini*, which is Latin for *in the year of our Lord*). Put these forms after the year being discussed, but leave a space. And do not add full stops. Don't use capitals for writing the name of a century or decade. So:

55 BC, 1877 AD, the second century BC, 18th century, the sixties

Deciding When to Use Numerals

Obviously, when you write addresses, phone numbers and dates, you're going to use figures (or numerals). That's pretty obvious. What's not so obvious is choosing whether to write other numbers in numerals or in words. The choice is a matter of style, not of grammar.

For example, the preferred style of the *For Dummies* series is to use numerals for numbers above ten. So if we go just a little higher, we get to 11. Some organisations elect to use words for any number that can be expressed in fewer than three words. So they spell out one hundred (two words) but switch to figures for 101 (four words).

Australian style recommends that you spell out numbers below 100 if they're not a key focus of what you're writing, and use words up to nine and numbers thereafter if figures feature heavily in your document. So, if you're writing a novel, the likelihood that the text will be thick with numbers is slight and you can apply the 'words up to ninety-nine' rule. If, however, you're preparing a geography report of a survey conducted at a local farmers' market, you apply the 'words up to nine' rule. Whichever system you use, be consistent. Here are a couple of examples:

Of the 178 people surveyed, only 16 had attended more than 10 times before. ('words up to nine rule')

Of the eighty-seven people surveyed, only sixteen had attended more than ten times before. ('words up to ninety-nine rule')

The preceding pointers are style guides, not 'always' rules. Sometimes, you may have to break the rule in order for your sentence to be consistent. Consider the following sentence in that report of a farmers' market we mentioned earlier in this section:

INCONSISTENT: The 87 people who attended specifically to purchase homemade dim sims ate an average of three each.

CONSISTENT: The 87 people who attended specifically to purchase homemade dim sims ate an average of 3 each.

ALSO CONSISTENT: The eighty-seven people who attended specifically to purchase homemade dim sims ate an average of three each.

Similarly, if a number begins a sentence, you must use words. And try to avoid ending a sentence with a numeral as well. You may also need to write out a fraction (for example, *four-fifths*) or any number that's an approximation (for example, *about three hundred*).

Chapter 10

Reporting Speech and Quoting Others

*P*unctuation is often a matter of style rather than grammar. In this chapter, we tell you how to handle quotations and punctuate speech in the simplest way acceptable here in the Land of Oz. We also explain how to use 'scare quotes' correctly in your writing (that's what you call those quotation marks people make in the air with their fingers).

Writing Conversation: Quotation Marks

Knowing the way to punctuate speech is important. Quite a few rules are involved and, if you read things that have been published in the US or the UK, you'll find different styles are used in each country. So we're going to give you the easiest and most consistent Aussie way.

When you learned this kind of punctuation at primary school, you may have called them *talking marks*. You'll also find them referred to as *inverted commas*, *quotation marks* or the shortened form of the latter, *quotes*.

First, you need to be clear about the difference between when the exact words spoken are recorded (direct speech) and when they're just reported (indirect speech).

Indicating indirect speech

Indirect speech tells you about a conversation, but it doesn't give people's exact words. It's a report of their ideas, but not a record of the words actually spoken or written, and it needn't use any of their own words. The rules for punctuating indirect speech are the same as the rules for text in general:

> Mrs Robinson, who lives next door to the accused, spoke to our reporter after the arrest. She said she is shocked by recent events, and expressed her sympathy for the victim of the alleged crime. Mrs Robinson claims that the whole community has been greatly upset by the events.

Dealing with direct speech

The following are examples of *direct speech*:

> 'It'll be lonely for you when Natasha moves interstate.'

> 'Yes, I expect it will.'

> 'But it'll be a relief knowing that she's not going to blow something up with one of her experiments.'

> 'That's true. I always feel safer when she's in one of her non-nuclear phases.'

We're quoting the speakers' exact words. You need to notice three important things about these examples.

The first thing is that single quotation marks are used. The argument about single or double is one of style. Newspaper style generally uses doubles, whereas most novels and magazines use singles. Who's right? Or maybe the question should be, 'Who's least wrong?' The trend in Australian style is to minimise punctuation (to use the minimum amount necessary). So, single quotation marks are preferred in Australia. (The KISS principle applies to punctuation as to so many other aspects of life — Keep It Simple Stupid!)

The second thing you need to notice is that in direct speech, such as the examples at the start of this section, the end punctuation of the words spoken always (*always*) goes *inside* the quotation marks. It could be a full stop, an exclamation mark or a question mark, but put it inside the quotation marks. Like this:

> 'What will you do when Natasha's gone?'

> 'I'll be able to eat chips in the bath undisturbed!'

The question mark and exclamation mark are helpful in telling you how the speakers are saying the words. That seems simple enough. ***Note:*** An *always* rule is a bonus in a grammar filled with exceptions and unusual cases.

Now for the third thing you need to notice. In each of the example sentences, the direct speech forms the entire sentence. This is not always the case with direct speech. The following section looks at what happens when other words are added.

Being formal with carrier expressions

Sometimes other words are used to form a sentence that contains direct speech. Like this:

'Might I ask your reasons?' he growled.

I replied from the other side of his vast desk, 'Well, sir, I just thought it was a good idea'.

'That', he said, 'was clearly not your best thought'.

An expression in a sentence that carries a piece of direct speech is called (... drum roll ... gasp of expectation ...) a *carrier expression*. Yep, you can breathe easy. You're not going to burst any brain cells trying to remember that clever little tag. The bit that might cause just the tiniest bit of brain strain, however, comes when we talk about punctuating carrier expressions. According to acceptable Australian style for formal writing, especially non-fiction writing, when the direct speech is attached to a carrier expression, the full stop comes at the end of the complete sentence — which means putting the full stop outside the quotation marks, as in the sample conversation at the start of this section. (For more information on formal language, refer to Chapter 1.)

Sorry, but more rule-related brain injury is yet to come. Look at these sentences:

She screamed, 'I don't believe you!'

Politely he enquired, 'Would you believe me?'

If you apply the carrier expression rule, each of the preceding sample sentences would have a full stop at the end of it because the direct speech is attached to a carrier expression. That would give you one punctuation point at the end of the quotation (an exclamation mark or a question mark) and another at the end of the entire sentence (a full stop). But putting two separate punctuation marks at the end of one sentence would be punctuation maximisation — the opposite of minimisation and of the KISS principle. So, when two types of end punctuation could occur together, choose the stronger one. Exclamation marks and question marks are stronger than full stops. Put the exclamation mark or question mark inside the quotation mark and omit the full stop at the end of the expression.

To recap this style for formal English, if the entire sentence is a piece of direct speech, put the end punctuation inside the quotation marks. If the direct speech is attached to a carrier expression and is an ordinary statement, put the final punctuation at the very end of the entire expression. If the direct speech ends the sentence and is a question or an exclamation, put the end punctuation inside the quotation mark.

Now for the good news. In informal writing and in fiction, these rules about end punctuation with carrier expressions are rarely applied. All the end punctuation, no matter whether the direct speech is a statement, a question or an exclamation, goes inside the final quotation marks. Phew! So, unless you're writing something formal — such as a report or an assignment — you can ignore the carrier expression rule and opt for the easier 'always' rule. Always put the end punctuation inside the closing quotation marks whether you're writing a carrier expression or not — like we do in this book.

Which sentence is correct for formal English?

A. Professor Pompous proclaimed, 'Despite requests, next week's lecture on the mating call of the Scarlet-sided Pobblebonk will not be held in a swamp'.

B. Professor Pompous proclaimed, 'Despite requests, next week's lecture on the mating call of the Scarlet-sided Pobblebonk will not be held in a swamp.'

Answer: Sentence A is correct, because a carrier expression is used so the full stop is outside the quotation marks. Sentence B would be correct for informal English.

Putting the speaker first

This and the following two sections look at different ways of putting the direct speech into a carrier sentence, starting with what happens when you put speakers before their words. And remember, we're applying the 'always' rule here (refer to preceding section for more).

Cynthia moaned, 'Nobody ever misses me.'

Natasha smiled, 'Well, we might if you ever went anywhere!'

Note that we've put a comma before the opening quotation mark and that the direct speech begins with a capital letter. (Newspapers generally use a colon instead of a comma to introduce direct speech, and some writers prefer a colon if the speech is long, but you don't have to bother. Stick to an 'always' rule and you can't go wrong.)

Putting the speaker last

If you put the information about who's speaking after the speech, you move the full stop to the end of your whole sentence (which will, of course, now be outside the quotes) and replace it with some other punctuation: a comma, question mark or exclamation mark. Everything else remains unchanged.

> 'Yes,' said her sister without looking up from her newspaper.
>
> 'Yes?' queried her sister without looking up from her newspaper.
>
> 'Yes!' agreed her sister without looking up from her newspaper.

Note especially that no capital letter is used after the comma (as you'd expect), but a capital letter isn't used after the question mark or exclamation mark either. You may think this is odd. Exclamation marks and question marks end sentences, so there should be a capital letter, right? Wrong! This is just one of the peculiarities of the rules with speech. These punctuation marks are regarded as indicating tone of voice rather than the end of the sentence (which comes where the full stop is).

Putting the speaker in the middle

Sometimes the information about who is speaking lands in the middle of a sentence:

> 'It's a great relief,' Chandra said, 'that I don't have to convince Cynthia to stay tonight.'

In this sentence, the speech is interrupted to tell you who's speaking. Right there in the middle, we've added

> , Chandra said,

Here are the rules for interruptions to sentences.

Rule 1: Nothing about the original speech changes. A capital letter isn't used at the start of the second half. But two more quotation marks must be used so that you still know which words are being spoken and which are just telling you who's speaking.

Rule 2: The interruption has to have a pair of commas, and the second comma goes at the end of the interruption.

Rule 3: The first comma always goes *inside* the quotation marks as though it's part of the first half of the speech.

Note that, in the interrupted quotations in this section, the quoted material adds up to only one sentence even though it's written in two separate parts.

Take care when writing direct speech that you don't create a run-on sentence. A *run-on sentence* is actually two sentences that have been stuck together (that is, *run* together) with nothing legal to join them. Even in direct speech you must obey the rules about joining sentences or both your computer and your reader could become confused. Check out these examples:

> WRONG: 'I don't understand why you're so soft on Damian,' complained Ellie, 'he's so unreliable.'

> RIGHT: 'I don't understand why you're so soft on Damian,' complained Ellie. 'He's so unreliable.'

The spoken material forms two complete sentences:

> SENTENCE 1: I don't understand why you're so soft on Damian.

> SENTENCE 2: He's so unreliable.

Because the spoken material forms two complete sentences, you must write two separate sentences. If you cram this quoted material into one sentence, you create a run-on sentence error.

To check for a run-on sentence, remove the information about who's speaking and check the spoken material. What's left? Enough for half a sentence? That's okay. A speech doesn't need to express a complete thought. Enough material for one sentence? Also okay. Enough material for two sentences? Not okay, unless you write two sentences.

Which is correct?

> **A.** 'You are grounded until I say otherwise,' said Dr Mackenzie to her son, Angus. 'I'm sorry it's come to this, but it's for your own good.'

> **B.** 'You are grounded until I say otherwise,' said Dr Mackenzie to her son, Angus, 'I'm sorry it's come to this, but it's for your own good.'

Answer: Sentence A is correct. The quoted material forms two complete sentences and you must quote it that way. Sentence 1 = *You are grounded until I say otherwise*. Sentence 2 = *I'm sorry it's come to this, but it's for your own good*.

Including speech within speech

People don't just talk *to* each other; they also talk *about* each other. They recount stories and repeat what so-and-so said about such-and-such — like this:

> Bill said, 'Mildred had the nerve to say my galahs are upsetting her snakes!'

Well, that's okay, but what if Bill wants to include Mildred's exact words? You need some more quotation marks:

> Bill said, 'Mildred had the nerve to say, "Your galahs are upsetting my snakes!"'

A sentence like this has to be sorted out. The first rule is that, as you're using single quotation marks to start with, you use double quotes for the inner speech.

Commas and end punctuation follow the same general rules in both double and single quotations. But, when you're quoting a complete sentence (inside another piece of direct speech), you should only put the appropriate end punctuation at the end of the sentence you're quoting. Look at the sentence in layers, working from the inside out, and then get rid of any duplicated end punctuation.

Asking questions within questions

If a sentence includes quoted words and the whole sentence is a question but the quoted words aren't, the question mark goes outside the quote marks. (Imagine giving both parts their punctuation and then deciding which to keep. A question mark or exclamation mark is more informative than a full stop, so it's stronger. That's the one to keep.)

> STEP 1 (WRONG): Did I hear that right? Did you just say, 'I don't like chocolate.'?
>
> STEP 2 (LOSE THE FULL STOP): Did I hear that right? Did you just say, 'I don't like chocolate'?
>
> STEP 1 (WRONG): Yes. I said, 'I don't like chocolate.'!
>
> STEP 2 (LOSE THE FULL STOP): Yes. I said, 'I don't like chocolate'!

But, for those rare occasions when both the quoted words and the sentence are questions or exclamations, put the question mark or exclamation mark inside the quotation marks. (Imagine giving both their punctuation to start with and then keeping one. One placed outside the quotes stands for the whole sentence only, as in the preceding examples. But one placed inside does double duty for both — just as a full stop in speech always does. So that's the one you keep.) Here's an example:

> STEP 1 (WRONG): Did Damian really ask Alice, 'Why do you eat rabbit food?'?

> STEP 2 (LOSE THE SPARE OUTSIDE QUESTION MARK. RIGHT): Did Damian really ask Alice, 'Why do you eat rabbit food?'

> STEP 1 (WRONG): Yes! And, when she tried to defend her choice to be a vegetarian, he said, 'Oh, get a life!'!

> STEP 2 (LOSE THE SPARE OUTSIDE EXCLAMATION MARK. RIGHT): Yes! And, when she tried to defend her choice to be a vegetarian, he said, 'Oh, get a life!'

Which sentence is correct?

A. He complained, 'She said to me, 'You're impossible!''

B. He complained, 'She said to me, "You're impossible!"'

C. He complained, 'She said to me, "You're impossible"'!

Answer: Sentence B is correct. You must enclose *You're impossible* in a different style of quotation marks from the larger statement, *She said to me you're impossible*. The exclamation mark at the end of the sentence goes inside both marks because it can apply to both.

Showing a change of speaker

In a conversation (as opposed to an earbashing), people take turns speaking. Take a look at this extremely mature discussion:

> 'You sat on my tuna sandwich,' Lucinda said.

> 'No, I didn't,' Martin said.

> 'Yes, you did,' Lucinda said.

> 'Did not!' Martin said.

> 'Did too!' Lucinda said.

Note that every time the speaker changes, we start a new paragraph, which makes the conversation easy to follow; the reader always knows who's talking.

Here's another version of the tuna sandwich fight:

> 'You sat on my tuna sandwich,' Lucinda said.
>
> 'No, I didn't,' Martin replied.
>
> 'Yes, you did.'
>
> 'Did not!'
>
> 'Did too!'

Sounds better, doesn't it? You can figure out who's speaking because of the paragraph breaks, so we can leave out a lot of boring repeated information about who's speaking.

So the rule is this: every change of speaker is signalled by a new paragraph.

You may have read some novels in which the author and editor have decided to break away from the traditional rules for punctuating direct speech and to keep the punctuation so clean and simple that they use no quotation marks at all. (James Joyce, as far back as 1914, called quotation marks 'perverted commas'.) Starting a new line for a new speaker is critical to this style, because it's often the only clue readers get that somebody is speaking. We're not suggesting you don't use quotation marks just yet. But, if you follow all the advice in this chapter, you'll be able to have a deep and meaningful discussion with your publisher about postmodern fashion in quotation marks when you're working out the details of your first book deal!

A new paragraph signals each speaker change, no matter how short the speeches. This rule applies even if the argument deteriorates into single-word statements such as

> 'Yes!'
>
> 'No!'

This rule also applies if a speech is interrupted:

> 'No, I didn't,' Martin said. He paused to think for a moment. No, he had no recollection of sitting on a sandwich. 'No, I'm sure I didn't.'

We didn't start a new paragraph for *'No, I'm sure I didn't'* because it's still Martin talking. If each new sentence is on a new line, a reader might think it is Lucinda speaking and become totally confused about who is saying what.

Remember the rule: Every change of speaker is signalled by a new paragraph. Don't start a new paragraph if no change of speaker has occurred.

All potential novelists please take note: Even a speech that's several paragraphs long must begin with an opening quotation mark and end with a closing quotation mark. *Don't* put a closing quotation mark at the end of any paragraph within the speech. (The reader will think the next paragraph is a different person speaking.) You can, if you wish, begin each new paragraph with an opening quotation mark (to remind the reader that it's still part of the speech), but this is not essential. When the quotation is finished (at the end of the last paragraph), put the closing quotation mark.

Writing someone's thoughts

Humans have a little voice inside their heads, like a running commentary on the world that continues pretty much all day. Right now you're hearing a little voice saying, 'What? I don't have a little voice in my head! That's crazy.' See, you *do* have a little voice inside your head. It's your thoughts, the voice that punctuates your day! To create believable characters in fiction, you need to represent their thoughts as well as their words. So how do you punctuate a character's thoughts? Should you use quotation marks (as we did for the little voice we imagined running through your head)? Should you use italics?

Guess what? No single answer to that question is possible. But we're not going to leave you completely in the dark. We do have some advice that can help you, so listen up.

If your piece contains a lot of direct speech, using quotation marks for thoughts becomes very messy. Situations will occur where you'll need to use double quotation marks inside single quotation marks and, before too long, you're in punctuation overload. Similarly, using italics can make the text look very busy and alienate your reader. The best way to indicate thoughts is to leave them as plain text. Your reader will soon know what is direct speech and what is thought. The following conversation between Jeremy and his father demonstrates this for you:

> 'Your mother and I value your views. You know that, don't you, son?'
>
> Sure. That's why my opinion about whether to go to Bali or Tasmania made such a difference that we spent four weeks looking at convict ruins and apple orchards. 'Yes, Dad.'
>
> 'Well, Jeremy, something big is about to happen.'
>
> 'Are we moving again?' That'd be right. Just when I'm actually enjoying being at school and I've found a way to handle that cranky neighbour who hates Metallica.

Recording Titles

Sometimes in your writing, you may need to record the name of a magazine, the headline of a newspaper article, the title of a song or film and so on. It's important to show the reader which words are part of the title, so they need to be separated from the text in some way. You have two ways to do this:

1. **Put the title in quotation marks.** This is the usual way to indicate titles of smaller works or parts of a whole.

2. **Set the title off from the rest of the writing with italics.** Titles of larger works or complete works are treated in this way.

Use quotation marks for the titles of

- Chapters
- Individual episodes of a television series
- Magazine and newspaper articles
- Poems
- Short stories and essays
- Songs

Use italics for the titles of

- Books and collections of poetry, stories and essays
- Magazines and newspapers
- Recorded works of art such as musical albums and DVDs
- Television programs, plays and films

Also use italics for the names of specific paintings and sculptural works, ships, aircraft, trains and other vehicles.

Here are some examples of quotation marks and italics for titles:

- 'A thousand dodgy deductions' (a newspaper article) in *Revenue News* (a newspaper)
- 'Ode to the tax man' (a poem) in *Economic E-coli* (an anthology of poetry)
- 'The self-assessment blues' (a song title) on *Me and My Taxes* (an album containing many songs)

✔ 'On the art of negative gearing' (an essay) in *Getting Rich and Staying Rich* (a magazine)

✔ 'Small business expenses' (an individual episode) on *The World of Taxation* (a television series).

You may be wondering which letters you should capitalise in a title. A useful general rule is that anything that's in italics can have a capital letter on every important word, including the first and last word, important or not. Anything in quotation marks usually has only one capital letter, at the start of the title. (For more information on capitalisation, refer to Chapter 9.)

Add quotation marks and italics to the following paragraph.

> Rob slumped slowly into his chair as the teacher read The homework manifesto aloud in class. Rob's essay, expressing his heartfelt dislike of any and all assignments, was never intended for his teacher's eyes. Rob had hidden the essay inside the cover of his textbook, The Land and People of Continents You Never Heard Of. Sadly, the textbook company, which also publishes The Most Boring Mathematics Possible, had recently switched to thinner paper, and the essay was clearly visible. The teacher ripped the essay from Rob's desperate hands. He hadn't been so embarrassed since the publication of his poem I hate homework in the school magazine, Happy Thoughts.

Answer: Put 'The homework manifesto' and 'I hate homework' in quotation marks because they're titles of an essay and a poem. Italicise *The Land and People of Continents You Never Heard Of* and *The Most Boring Mathematics Possible* and *Happy Thoughts* because they're titles of books and a magazine.

Quoting Someone Else

A *quotation* is a repetition of someone else's written or spoken words — just one word or a whole statement or passage. You see quotations in almost all forms of writing.

When a quotation consists of a few words but not a complete sentence, you can put these words inside the very appropriately named *quotation marks* in a sentence of your own. If you're quoting whole sentences, it's a bit more complicated. Here are the rules:

✔ Put a short quotation of complete sentences (up to about three lines) inside quotation marks within the text of whatever you are writing.

✔ Indent and single-space a longer quotation, with space above and below it, so that it looks like a separate block of print. Such quotations are called *displayed* quotations or *block* quotes.

✔ Use the block quote format to indicate the lines of a poem when writing about poetry.

Here's an example of a *block quote* from an imaginary book:

> Witherby, in his paper 'Why Homework is Useless', makes the following point:

> A study of 1,000 students reveals that those who have no time to rest are not as efficient as those who do. Teens surveyed all indicated that sleeping is more valuable than homework, as is listening to music, talking with friends on the phone or computer and watching television.

Quote or *quotation*? Strictly speaking, *quote* is what you do (in other words, it's the verb *to quote*), and a *quotation* is the text you're quoting (thus a noun — so you *quote* a *quotation*). Technically, the punctuation marks you use to indicate the quotation are called *quotation marks*. In conversational English, *quote* and *quotation* have long been interchangeable. The difference between the two words is being lost; now, you'll find *quote marks* used even in some formal grammar references.

Punctuating Quotations

The simplest way to punctuate a block quotation is to introduce each one with a colon (as we have in the preceding section). You're allowed to do this whether the text before the quotation is a complete sentence or not.

Note that we didn't use any quotation marks around the example in the preceding section. That's because the space around the quotation shows that you're quoting, so quotation marks are unnecessary.

When a quotation is not set as a block, you can't leave the quotation marks out because you need to show where the words you're quoting begin and end:

> Witherby notes that 'Teens surveyed all indicated that sleeping is more valuable than homework'.

You need to note three important things here. One is the capital *T* in the middle of the sentence. It's necessary because a capital letter is used at the start of the quotation. Another is the absence of a colon.

A colon isn't needed when you include someone else's words in your sentence. And, finally, the full stop is outside the quotation marks. The words quoted come from inside one of Witherby's sentences, not at the end with a full stop. So, the full stop belongs at the conclusion of the whole sentence.

Sometimes, you may not want or need to use every word in a quotation. Look at this:

> Witherby goes on to say that 'When 1,000 teens were surveyed, they all indicated that ... listening to music ... and watching television' were 'more valuable than schoolwork'.

For our purpose, some words aren't relevant, so we've put three dots to show we've left something out. The dots tell our readers that we've done this, and they can check the original text if they want to see what we've left out. (These little dots are called *ellipses* or *ellipsis points*. Don't change the channel. You can find more information on ellipses in the next section.)

The other important thing to note is that sometimes we don't seem to have a full stop for our own sentence. That's because we don't need two full stops. If what you're quoting concludes with a full stop, you have to make a choice. These are both correct:

> He goes on to say that 'Teens ... indicated that sleeping is more valuable than homework, as is listening to music, talking with friends ... and watching television.' (We've used Professor Witherby's full stop and let it end our sentence as well.)

> He goes on to say that 'Teens ... indicated that sleeping is more valuable than homework, as is listening to music, talking with friends ... and watching television'. (We've left out the professor's full stop — ending the quotation just one tiny dot too early — and used our own full stop to end the whole sentence.)

Professor Witherby has written you a letter in which he says, 'Dr Jones raises some interesting issues in his kind review of my book. He has been very generous in his appraisal of my argument'. Which of these are correct?

A. Professor Witherby says in his letter that 'Dr Jones raises some interesting issues in his kind review'.

B. Professor Witherby says in his letter that 'Dr Jones raises some interesting issues in his ... review.'

C. Professor Witherby says in his letter that Dr Jones's review raises some 'interesting issues.'

D. Professor Witherby says in his letter that 'Dr Jones raises some interesting issues in his kind review of my book.'.

Answer: Sentence A is correct because it quotes part of a sentence from the letter and puts the full stop outside the quotation marks.

Sentence B is wrong. The ellipsis is fine: the writer doesn't want to include the flattery, and has used the ellipsis to show that something has been left out. But the end of the sentence is also missing and the full stop is inside the quote marks, suggesting this was the end of the sentence. The full stop must go outside the quotation marks.

Sentence C is also wrong because the full stop is inside the quote marks. It's okay to pick out the significant words and put them in quote marks. (This avoids the sort of problem that sentence B got around by using the ellipsis.) However, the quoted words didn't end the sentence, so the full stop should again go outside the quotation marks.

Sentence D is wrong too. You can't have the full stop in the quote and another to end the sentence. It's overkill.

Joining the Dots with Ellipses

An ellipsis is a punctuation mark of three dots. As shown in the examples in the preceding section, it is generally used to show that some words have been left out of a text or speech:

> Smith said: 'The war was fought on many fronts ... with final surrender in late spring.'

When you're quoting someone else's words, you can't leave bits out without saying so. It's just plain rude! So place three dots (and only three dots — never five or six or more) wherever you've left out words from the original. When multiple sets are used, the dots are called *ellipses*. (One set is an *ellipsis*.)

If you delete the end of a sentence, don't use four dots. Omit the full stop. You can, however, add an exclamation mark or question mark before or after an ellipsis. You'll see ellipses with and without spaces around them. Aussie style is to put a space before and after an ellipsis.

Have a look at Ingrid's description of what she did last night, as written in her diary. The parts that she'll leave out when she explains to her teacher why she hasn't done her homework are in italics:

> I sat down at the computer last night to write the essay. I truly love writing essays, *not,* and I certainly want to do well in this class *if I can get good grades without doing a stitch of work.* I began to write shortly before eight o'clock, but *the phone rang almost immediately. I spoke with my friends for no more than three hours. Then my mother asked me if I wanted a snack. I said yes. I ate two or three large pizzas and settled down at the computer. Then* my stomach hurt, and I was very tired. I had to go to bed. I'll do the essay tonight.

And here's the edited version, punctuated with ellipses:

> I sat down at the computer last night to write the essay. I truly love writing essays ... and I certainly want to do well in this class ... I began to write shortly before eight o'clock, but ... my stomach hurt, and I was very tired. I had to go to bed. I'll do the essay tonight.

All the ellipses have three dots with a space either side ... The third ellipsis covers a multitude of sins — whole sentences missing plus a bit of a sentence. Using an ellipsis connects the remaining text on both sides of the deleted text so it is read as if it were a connected sentence.

By omitting some of the information, Ingrid's being dishonest and you shouldn't follow her example! One of the most important issues in writing is credibility. If you change the meaning of what you're quoting by leaving out crucial details, your readers will figure this out eventually, and then they won't trust anything you say. (Also, your teacher may fail you.) Check the passage you're quoting before and after you've cut it. Do both convey the same message? If not, don't cut it (or cut differently).

An ellipsis can also be used to indicate a pause in speech or an unfinished thought. This can show hesitation or indecision, particularly in dialogue:

> I mean ... well ... let me think.

> I don't know what to do about that bill! It's already overdue ...
> I shouldn't have ... I just don't have ... What am I going to do?

Beware: Using ellipses in this way can get really annoying really quickly. Don't overdo it.

Putting Brackets within Quotations

You're probably familiar with round brackets, which are called *parentheses* (such as shown here). But, when you're quoting something and adding words of your own in the middle of the quotation, you use *square brackets* to let the reader know that these words weren't part of the original. For example, if we were reporting that Charlotte had written in her essay about Einstein that the 20th century (as we know it) began with the five papers he wrote in 1905, we'd do it like this:

> Charlotte wrote in her essay that 'the 20th century (as we know it) began with the five papers that he [Einstein] wrote in 1905'.

Charlotte wrote *(as we know it)*, including the parentheses, but she didn't write the word *Einstein*; she wrote *he*. We had to add *[Einstein]* so that you'd know who she was talking about.

The word most commonly added to quotations using square brackets in this way is *sic*. This is Latin for *thus* (or *Don't blame us for this mistake — it's in the original*). For example:

> Lucinda wrote in her history essay that 'Mary Queen of Scots went to her cousin Elizabeth for refuse [*sic*]'.

Lucinda meant *refuge*, but that's not what she wrote. We put the *[sic]* in so that you'd know it was Lucinda's mistake, not a spelling mistake in this book. These brackets are always square, and *sic* is in italics to show that it isn't an English word.

Part III
Polishing Your Writing and Comprehension

Top Five Ways to Improve Your Reading Comprehension

- **Consider the literal facts and details:** Literal facts and details are clearly stated in a text. Sometimes you'll need to look at and recall specific facts and details within one sentence. Other times, you may need to search for facts and details in more than one sentence, or the text as a whole.

- **Use prior knowledge to interpret texts:** Interpreting texts means making a prediction or a 'best guess' about what might happen. To do this, you can use your background knowledge and prior experiences, and facts and knowledge gained from other sources, such as friends, movies, websites and other texts.

- **Identify the main idea and structure:** Explicit main ideas are clearly stated (sometimes using a topic sentence) while implicit main ideas aren't clearly stated — so you need to identify them using clues such as synonyms, repeated words and topic organisation. The structure of a text is the ways ideas have been organised, and outlines the sequence of events.

- **Separate fact from opinion:** A *fact* is a statement that can be proven to be true. An *opinion* is a statement that is a personal point of view or judgement.

- **Use context clues:** These are signals within words, sentences and paragraphs. Sometimes you can use context clues within words to help with word meanings. You can also use context clues to increase your understanding of the whole text from the sentence structure, figurative language or by reading around a word.

Part III

Polishing Your Writing
and Comprehension

In this part . . .

- ✔ Organise your ideas and ensure your writing flows, is cohesive, and uses strong, effective language.

- ✔ Expand your vocabulary and understand literary devices such as metaphor, analogy and irony.

- ✔ Get more out of the texts you read by improving your comprehension.

- ✔ Battle your spelling demons and spell more confidently.

Chapter 11

Writing with Cohesion and Coherence

*L*earning the nitty-gritty of grammar initiates you into the universal clan of language lovers. Welcome. It also helps you to correct your errors or, better yet, to avoid making errors at all. That's wonderful. In this chapter, however, we stride bravely up to the junction of good grammar and good writing style and examine how the two are inextricably connected.

Creating Writing That Flows: Cohesion

Have you ever been frustrated because even though you've included all the required information in your essay and you're satisfied with the content, your piece still seems awkward and a bit disjointed — more like a bus trip than a ride in a luxury vehicle? Fear not; help is at hand. With understanding of how to create better connectedness, your writing can flow with the smooth ease of a Ferrari.

For a wordsmith, *cohesion* refers to the way whole sentences and paragraphs are linked to each other. In a cohesive piece of writing, the sentences and paragraphs build on each other and grow in a logical way. Ideas flow and the reader can follow your message effortlessly. In the following sections, we cover sequencing and linking ideas.

Putting ideas in order: Sequencing

How hard can it be to get your ideas in the right order? Well, sometimes that's exactly what stumps writers. The best way to sequence and link information is from old or known information to new. Then, the new information at the end of one sentence becomes the old information for the sentence that follows, like this:

> William Dampier was very curious about what the world beyond England was like. *He* was *also curious* about plants, animals and the people he met on his travels. Observations about *these things* filled his journals.

The second sentence builds on the information in the first sentence by substituting *he* for William Dampier, using the connecting word *also* to connect ideas, and repeating the word *curious*. Then, the words *these things* link the third sentence to the second sentence by summarising the words *plants, animals and the people he met*. That's *cohesion* at a sentence level.

Cohesion of paragraphs creates the structure for a piece of writing. The best way to do this depends on what you're writing. Here are some logical ways to sequence ideas:

- Past to present to future
- General to specific
- Simple to complicated
- Best to worst
- Ideal to actual
- Problem to solution
- Question to answer
- Idea to example
- Data or findings to conclusions

Think about what you're writing and why, and then choose a suitable technique to put your ideas in order. If you're writing a report for science, you may move from findings to conclusions, whereas for a short story, you could opt for a chronological (then until now) approach.

Connecting ideas with transition words

Like a story that's impossible to put down, or an argument that's so logical it changes what you've always thought, good writers link the ideas in their sentences and connect their sentences into paragraphs that lead to a logical conclusion. One of the ways they do this is with *signpost words*, sometimes also called *transition words*, such as *therefore*, *apparently*, *similarly*, *finally*. They signal the relationships between ideas to help readers navigate the document. Here's an example with the transition words in italics:

> Cat-lovers have many reasons for preferring cats to dogs. *Firstly*, feline friends are quieter than canine companions, *thus* far less annoying to neighbours. And *secondly*, cats are infinitely cleaner than dogs. *After all*, you don't have to carry poo bags around when you have a cat or bathe them to eliminate their dreadful smell.
>
> *By contrast*, dog defenders argue that cats don't prevent burglaries or protect vehicles. *Furthermore*, cats cause much discomfort to allergy sufferers. *In fact*, very few people find themselves wheezing and sneezing in the presence of dogs; *however*, the allergen in cat spit affects millions.

Notice how commas and/or semicolons accompany the signpost words. They are like extra links added to a chain of words (the sentence) and, if you remove them, the meaning is unchanged.

Table 11-1 shows signpost words can help you create logical links in your writing.

Table 11-1	Signpost Words
Link Required	*Words to Choose*
Adding to or continuing	additionally, again, also, as well as, besides, coupled with, furthermore, in addition to this, in the same way, moreover, too
Comparing	by comparison, correspondingly, in the same way, likewise, moreover, similarly
Showing cause or consequence	accordingly, as a result, consequently, for this reason, hence, therefore, thus
Contrasting	alternatively, by contrast, conversely, despite that, even though, instead, nevertheless, on the contrary, on the other hand, otherwise, rather
Showing chronology	afterward, during, earlier, first of all, following that, formerly, later on, meanwhile, next, previously, secondly, simultaneously, subsequently, the next step, to begin with
Giving examples or explaining	exemplifying this, for example, for instance, including, indeed, in fact, in particular, namely, specifically, such as, that is, thus, to illustrate
Showing exceptions	apart from, aside from, barring, excluding, other than, with the exception of
Summarising or concluding	after all, all in all, finally, in any case, in conclusion, in short, on balance, on the whole, to sum up

Choose wisely from this list to connect your sentences into paragraphs and your paragraphs into longer pieces of writing. By doing so, you take your reader with you on the journey from start to finish.

Selecting from the words in the preceding chart, fill the gaps in this passage (marked with *X*):

> Predominantly carnivores, wild dogs also supplement their meat diet with berries, nuts and grasses. *X*, they absorb grains and grasses from the intestines of herbivores they eat. *X* feeding some cereal-based foods to your pet dog may be worthwhile. *X*, raw meat provides the best nutrients for your dog. *X* a vegetarian diet is not appropriate for man's best friend.

Answer: You could link these ideas in several ways, but here's a logical selection of signpost words to fill the gaps:

> Predominantly carnivores, wild dogs also supplement their meat diet with berries, nuts and grasses. *In addition to this*, they absorb grains and grasses from the intestines of herbivores they eat. *Therefore*, feeding some cereal-based foods to your canine companion may be worthwhile. *On the other hand*, raw meat provides the best nutrients for your pet dog; *consequently*, a vegetarian diet is not appropriate.

Being Absolutely Clear: Plain English

Few things are more frustrating than trying to decode a document that's so chock-a-block with technical words and long sentences that you have to read it several times to get the message. You want your reader to thank you for communicating with them, not curse you. Writing that speaks directly to the reader, and is clear and concise is described as *plain English*, and it's a perfect example of the overlap of style and grammar.

Plain English sentences are always written in *active voice* (active and passive voice are discussed in Chapter 3), are thoughtfully coordinated and subordinated (discussed in Chapter 4), and carefully punctuated. Whole books have been written about it; organisations are dedicated to it. Here, we provide a quick look at the basics of plain English.

Avoiding word-wasting

Having to write formal documents such as job applications, school reports and essays often brings on a bad case of verbal diarrhoea. It's a fair bet that one of the reasons for this is that people think wordy, ornate writing sounds formal in the way that legal documents do. In reality, using unnecessarily flowery language just sounds like pompous bafflegab. Plain English demands that you should never use more words than you need. Table 11-2 shows some examples of unnecessarily flowery language, and what they can be replaced with.

Table 11-2	Ways to Use Plain English
Unnecessary Language	*Replace With*
at the present moment	now
for the purpose of	for
in the event of	if
in the majority of circumstances	usually, generally, mostly
in respect of	about
make an application	apply
on account of the fact that	because
provide an explanation	explain
with the minimum of delay	immediately, quickly

And here are some flabby sentences with their plain language counterparts:

> WRONG: If there are any issues about which you require further information or particulars, I shall be glad to provide any additional details by telephone.

> RIGHT: Please call if you have any queries.

> WRONG: It is important for you to remember the limited capacity for attention of many members of the reading public and thus the relative importance of choosing words and sentence structures that fit together in a dynamic way to keep your audience's attention focused.

> RIGHT: Remember that readers bore easily, so choose dynamic words and sentence structures that engage your audience.

Sometimes the excess baggage in a document comes with *clichés* — expressions that are overused and dull. In fact, sometimes people communicate in expressions that are almost meaningless. Plain English is direct and fresh:

> WRONG: I write to place before you my application for the position of trainee Jedi knight as advertised in *The Galactic Times*.

RIGHT: As a huge fan of the Force, I dream of training as a Jedi knight.

WRONG: For the project we currently have on the front burner, it will be necessary to massage the material thoroughly before putting it to bed.

RIGHT: We will need to edit this project carefully.

Wordy documents waste people's time. Your reader (and your teacher marking you) won't get bogged down in a plain English success story because it communicates without being flowery or verbose.

Deciding when a sentence has too many words is like responding to the question, 'How long is a piece of string?' Answer: As long as it needs to be. The recommendation for plain Aussie English, however, is that if the average length of your sentences is more than 22 words, you're overdoing it. Pull back. A 15 to 20 word average is plenty.

Selecting the best words

You will have noticed that employing a functional interface benchmark (FIB) and leading-edge impactful energetics (LIE) can improve your base-level efficiency. You haven't? Well, of course not, because neither those gobbledygook word combinations nor the acronyms they form (FIB and LIE) exist. They do, however, demonstrate one of the enemies of plain English: trendy language and jargon. This is almost meaningless language often shared between people who work in the same field or share an interest. Plain English demands that everyone be able to understand your document, not just someone who thinks and speaks exactly as you do. Choose clear everyday words over complex specialised ones.

One of the most helpful, friendly features you have in your word processor is the thesaurus that just drops out of the tool bar at the click of a mouse. Or, if you prefer, you can make friends with a thesaurus in good old-fashioned book form. As we cover in Chapter 1, a thesaurus gives you alternatives to the words you've written (or are about to write), plus a range of similar words, and even opposites. Finding the exact word to express your meaning is that easy.

However, don't just throw in any word from the list your thesaurus suggests. You don't want to perturb your audience with an anomalous and expeditious permutation in your mode of interchange. Choose words that fit comfortably with the rest of your plain English piece.

See Chapter 12 for more help with your vocab skills.

Staying positive

Remaining positive is another feature of plain language — not positive as in your frame of mind but positive as in your word choice. Positive words are easier to understand because they require only one thought process; you don't have to think about what a word means and then work out the opposite meaning. Table 11-3 shows negative constructions and how they can be made positive.

Table 11-3	Negative versus Positive Constructions
Negative	*Positive*
fail to notice	overlook
not dissimilar	similar
not the same	different
unfinished	ongoing, continuing
untrue	false

And here's an example sentence, showing negative and then positive word choice:

> WRONG: Just under half of the team didn't know the address of the oval.

> RIGHT: Over half of the team knew the address of the oval.

Finally, don't use a noun where a verb would fit. Verbs communicate more clearly and make your writing livelier. The nouns and corresponding verbs are in italics in the following examples:

> WRONG: We need *clarification* of exactly what *improvements* will be made upon the *implementation* of your plan. (Notice that this is also in passive voice.)

> RIGHT: Please *clarify* exactly what you *will improve* when you *implement* your plan. (This version is in active voice.)

Being concise doesn't mean being brief. It means choosing the best word, using the active voice, and creating essays and other documents that are understood at first reading. Master plain English and that mark you dream of is much more likely to be yours. May the Force be with you!

Chapter 12

Building Vocabulary and Comprehension

*Y*our vocabulary is the total number of words that you know and use — and the wonderful thing about your vocabulary is that you can add to it all the time. You can improve your language skills through understanding how words are built or created, and the relationships between words. And once you understand how to use words accurately, you can start looking at the ways literary devices can enhance the language used in the texts you read — and start using these devices in your own writing. In this chapter, we take you through these building blocks of vocabulary and good writing.

We also look at ways you can improve your reading comprehension — in other words, the meaning you're getting out of the words you're reading. Your reading comprehension can be enhanced by understanding not only the main ideas, facts and structure the author is providing but also what prior knowledge you are bringing to the text. We provide some tips for increasing your skills in these areas, and finish the chapter by highlighting some techniques for connecting ideas.

Working on Your Vocabulary

The number of words in the English language is amazing — and, we admit, sometimes bewildering. But once you start to understand the way words are formed, and the relationships between words, you're well on your way to building your vocabulary and language skills — and your reading comprehension and writing will improve as a result.

Many words have *synonyms* (words with similar meanings) or *antonyms* (words with opposite meanings). Some words are easily confused. *Homographs* are spelled the same but are pronounced differently and have different meanings. *Homophones* sound the same but are spelled differently and have different meanings.

In the following sections, we get you up to speed on these types of words, and introduce you to some word relationships.

Sizing up synonyms and antonyms

Synonyms are words with similar meanings. For example, the words *start* and *begin* are synonyms. Of course, no word means exactly the same thing as another word, so choosing to replace a word with a synonym of that word will still change the meaning of your writing (however slightly) and perhaps other aspects as well, such as the rhythm and flow. So the synonym you choose to replace another word with will depend on the meaning you are trying to convey in a particular context.

Antonyms are words with opposite meanings — for example, *fast* is an antonym of *slow*, and vice versa. Antonyms are always connected in some way. In our example, fast and slow are connected by the topic of speed.

A synonym or antonym must always be the same part of speech or word class as the word it replaces — that is, a verb must replace a verb, a noun must replace a noun and so on.

Homing in on homographs and homophones

Homographs are words that have the same spelling but different pronunciation and different meanings. For example, *row*, rhyming with *toe*, means 'a line'; and *row*, rhyming with *how*, means 'a quarrel'. Another example is *bow* in your hair and *bow* to the queen. To avoid mispronouncing these types of words, you need to identify any homographs before reading a text aloud.

Homophones are words that have the same pronunciation but different meanings. For example, *roar* means 'to make a loud deep sound', while *raw* means 'not cooked'. Another example is '*You* are nice and the farmer has a *ewe*' (that's a sheep for the last one).

Homophones can trip you up when you're checking your work for correct spelling (and are unlikely to be identified by your word processor's spell checker, either). So you need to be able to identify them and check they are spelled correctly to match the intended meaning.

The following Tables 12-1 and 12-2 have some tricky words in them. Don't be scared — it just so happens that many homonyms and homographs are fairly sophisticated words. Some of the words are not for the fainthearted, but they will help you test both your vocabulary and your spelling (covered in more detail in Chapter 13).

Table 12-1 shows homographs — words that have two distinctly different meanings but nevertheless are spelled the same.

Table 12-1 A Gross of Homographs (Give or Take a Few Dozen)		
bass	bow	buffet
close	compound	converse
desert	does	dove
entrance	frequent	grave
gross	intimate	invalid
lame	lead	live
minute	nail	object
patient	polish	present
project	putting	record
refuse	resume	row
shower	sow	tear
tower	wind	wound

In case you're wondering about the dual meaning of some of these words, here are a few definitions:

- ✔ **Desert:** Either those dry arid places you wouldn't want to be lost in or how you can leave or *desert* a place.

- ✔ **Grave:** Either the kind in a cemetery or the very serious or *grave* situation.

- ✔ **Gross:** Either large or yuk or the old-fashioned measure.

✔ **Nail:** Either you have one on your finger or you *nail* down a job.

✔ **Patient:** You can be this either when you're waiting in line or when you're confined in a hospital.

Table 12-2 provides quite a few homophones to keep you going.

Table 12-2	A Hatful of Homophones	
aloud/allowed	ate/eight	blue/blew
board/bored	break/brake	buy/by
cereal/serial	deer/dear	for/four
groan/grown	hair/hare	hear/here
hole/whole	knot/not	lead/led
meet/meat	naval/navel	no/know
pain/pane	pair/pear	passed/past
patience/patients	peace/piece	plain/plane
principal/principle	rain/reign/rein	real/reel
rode/road/rowed	sale/sail	scene/seen
scent/sent/cent	seam/seem	see/sea
sew/so/sow	sight/site	some/sum
son/sun	steal/steel	straight/strait
symbol/cymbal	tail/tale	there/they're/their
threw/through	thrown/throne	tide/tied
to/too/two	wear/where	week/weak
whether/weather	who's/whose	witch/which
write/right		

Tackling word relationships

The relationships between words can be highlighted by word plays such as spoonerisms and idioms. Understanding these can sometimes be a bit tricky, particularly if English isn't your first language, but they can increase your reading pleasure and add flavour to your own writing.

Here's the lowdown on these playful words and expressions:

- ✔ **Collocation:** This is made up of two or more words used in combination that are an accepted part of our language. Some examples include 'tried and true', 'safe and sound', 'bacon and eggs', 'salt and pepper', 'a pack of lies' and 'catch a cold'.

- ✔ **Idiom:** This is a form of expression peculiar to a language. An idiom has a meaning other than its literal one. For example, 'It's raining cats and dogs' or 'That exam was a piece of cake'.

- ✔ **Malapropism:** This occurs when a word is used incorrectly but sounds very like the word that should have been used, usually for humorous effect. For example, 'The flood damage was so bad they had to evaporate (evacuate) the city'.

- ✔ **Spoonerism:** This occurs when the initial sounds of words are swapped around, again often for humorous effect. For example, 'I have joined a protest group who want to wave the sails (save the whales)'.

Looking at Literary Devices

Once you have more of a handle on the vocab basics, you can start to add some flair and depth to your writing using literary devices.

Some words are used figuratively — that is, they are used to make non-literal comparisons to extend their possible meanings. These are called *figures of speech* and include similes, metaphors and personification.

Other techniques include analogy and allusion, and irony and hyperbole.

Adding depth with simile, metaphor and symbolism

Understanding figures of speech helps you get more out of many different sorts of texts. And adding them to your own writing helps you add another layer of meaning.

A *simile* is a direct comparison of two different things. For example:

The traffic was like a crawling trail of insects.

My room was as hot as a pizza oven.

Similes can be recognised by the use of the words *like* and *as*.

A *metaphor* uses words to make a link between two unlike things. You can use metaphor to compare and connect different things without using *like* or *as*. For example:

> On the football field, he was a lion.

> My grandma is on the internet highway, in the slow lane.

Mixed metaphors occur when two or more metaphors are used to produce a mixture of ideas that do not fit together. For example:

> The tidal wave of support was a ray of sunshine in our darkest hour.

Personification is a special type of metaphor that treats objects or abstract ideas as if they have human qualities. For example:

> The sun smiled on the parade.

> Harry's idea was killed off and buried without a funeral.

Symbolism is a literary device where one thing is used to represent or suggest something else. For example:

- ✔ A dove is used as a symbol of peace.
- ✔ A heart or a red rose is used as a symbol of love.
- ✔ Night can be used as a symbol of darkness of the soul, or evil.

Pick which of the following sentences uses symbolism:

A. As her tears subsided, Maddie looked up to see the golden glow of the sun breaking through the clouds.

B. Jane's father has just had his life saved by open-heart surgery.

C. Memories of that wonderful summer spent with Geoff came flooding back to her.

D. Johnno sat in his camp, staring into the cold ashes of the fire and pondering the destruction of his grand plan.

Answer: The sentences that contain symbolism are A (the sun breaking through the clouds) and D (the cold ashes of the fire).

Adding analogy and allusion

You can also add depth to your writing through using analogy and allusion.

An *analogy* is a likeness between two or more things that forms the basis for a comparison. For example, an analogy may be drawn between a heart and a pump, or a child's brain and a sponge. A good way to create an analogy in your writing is to compare the way things function. For example, a pen's function is to write. A bed's function is to be used for sleeping.

An *allusion* is an indirect reference to something. It relies on the reader having the experience and the knowledge to understand the reference. The film *Shrek*, for example, contains many allusions to well-known nursery rhymes and fairytales.

Playing with irony, hyperbole and oxymoron

Devices such as irony, hyperbole and oxymoron may need a little work to get right (or even to pick up correctly when you're reading), but can help bring a piece to life.

Irony is a literary device in which the apparent meaning is the opposite of that intended, as is made clear by the context or tone. Irony can also be used to create a state of affairs or circumstances contrary to what is expected, and it is often used for humorous effect.

See if you can pick the irony in the following passage:

> After several days on the run, Paul was recaptured and returned to the high-security wing of the prison. Flanked by armed guards, he was told the new restrictions to which he would be subjected. 'Boss, you've got to stop being so good to me,' he said.

Answer: The final sentence in the piece contains irony — Paul's reaction is the opposite of what you would expect (and probably didn't go down so well with the guards).

Hyperbole is an exaggeration or overstatement used for effect and not intended to be taken literally. For example:

> This case weighs a tonne.

> I've told you a million times I'm not interested.

An *oxymoron* is a contradiction. For example:

Parting is such *sweet sorrow*.

We must make *haste slowly*.

Improving Your Reading Comprehension

Reading comprehension is the process of understanding what you read. *Read* is a verb that means 'to look at and understand' or 'to look at and say aloud' or 'to translate and understand'. These definitions suggest that real reading can't really happen without comprehension.

But when you comprehend what you read, you do so at different levels. At each level, the complexity of your thinking skills increases. You start at a *literal* level and move up to an *interpretive* level, a *critical* level and a *creative* level.

Considering the literal facts and details

Literal facts and details are clearly stated in a text. Think about a typical comprehension test in English. Questions will usually ask you to focus on the following:

- ✔ **How? When? Where? What? Which?** These types of questions are asking you to find information from the text.

- ✔ **Why?** This is asking you to find a reason from the text.

- ✔ **True or false?** Again, this question is asking you to find information from the text.

- ✔ **What do you think?** This question is asking you to give your opinion, in your own words.

So some questions about a text can be answered by recalling specific facts and details within one sentence. This sentence might be found within a paragraph of text. To answer the question in a test, you need to find the sentence that uses words matching those in the question and that answers exactly what the question asks.

To answer more advanced questions, you often have to think about the question and then search for facts and details in more than one sentence.

Sometimes, you can find facts and details by looking for cohesive ties. A *cohesive tie* is a word or phrase that marks a connection between sentences. Examples are synonyms, pronouns and numbers. Other clues might be topics, groups or categories.

Using prior knowledge to interpret texts

Part of interpreting texts as you read them means making a *prediction* or a 'best guess' about what might happen in the text. To do this, you can use clues from your own background knowledge or from your prior experiences in life. For example, facts and details that you already know from your life and prior experience outside the text can help you understand a text you are reading. You can recall things you have done in your life — that birthday party you hosted that ended terribly, for example — that can help you understand the text. You can also use facts and details you have learned from other sources, such as information from a friend, a movie or a website.

You can also gain knowledge for interpreting the text as you're reading it, using the background knowledge you learn as you read through a particular text to make later predictions. Background knowledge gained from other texts that you have already read on that same topic can also help you understand the text you're reading now.

Interpreting texts also involves making *inferences* or drawing reasonable conclusions about factual details that aren't clearly stated. Like when making predictions, you can again use your prior experience and background knowledge to make these judgements. You can make inferences across sentences by finding main ideas, distinguishing between fact and opinion, and using context clues (topics covered in the following sections).

Sometimes you can make inferences about feelings, tone or mood from vocabulary or figurative language.

Picking up on signal words

Signal words (or cue/clue words) can help you to understand how information is organised and provide clues about what is important. So picking up on them can help your reading comprehension.

For example, *because* is a signal word in the sentence 'Sacha didn't go to Cory's party because she had a bad case of the flu'. If you were asked the question 'Why didn't Sacha go to Cory's party?' you could answer it by using the information that comes after the signal word *because*.

Identifying the main idea and structure

To really understand texts, you may need to find the *main idea. Explicit* main ideas are clearly stated and tell you the most important ideas. In some texts, the explicit main idea is clearly stated in one sentence (lucky you!). This sentence is usually referred to as the *topic sentence.*

Implicit main ideas are not clearly stated (making things a bit tougher). Sometimes, texts include synonyms and repeated words. From these, you can write your own sentence about the most important idea. Other texts might include sentences that are all facts and details about the same topic, category or group. From this, you can use a topic, category or group name to write a sentence about the most important idea.

Another aspect of understanding texts is to be able to identify their structure — that is, the way ideas have been organised. A *sequence of events* is the order in which things happen. To find a sequence of events, you can seek out signal words (see the sidebar 'Picking up on signal words' for more).

Signal words such as *first, next* and *last* show a simple sequence of events. In texts with a simple sequence of events, signal words appear in the same order as the events are presented. Signal words such as *preceding, subsequently* and *ultimately* may show a more complex sequence of events. In texts with a complex sequence of events, signal words do not always appear in the same order as the events occur. But don't let this deter you! By thinking about how the signal words are used, you can work out the sequence of events. And remember — signal words can begin a sentence or they can occur within a sentence.

To understand and easily recall factual texts, authors often provide a *summary* or outline. This is a clearly stated central idea that combines main ideas from several paragraphs or sections. Some factual texts contain a summary that is clearly stated at the start, while other factual texts help you find or write the summary by using text elements such as bolded words, headings and subheadings.

In narrative texts such as novels, graphic novels and short stories, summaries can be constructed from the main events that develop the story. The summary may be of the main plot or the themes, or about the characters' actions, thoughts and feelings.

How do visual elements support written texts?

In your quest to understand texts more fully, you may need to look at the visual elements that accompany the words. Common visuals include pictures, diagrams, charts, maps and comic strips. These might provide similar, different or more information about the words you read. This means some visuals support or add information to the words you read, while other visuals don't support the words you read.

Separating fact from opinion

Sometimes separating fact from opinion can be hard — but sometimes it can be easy. (As in, 'Lucinda just spent $250 on a dress' (fact) versus 'She really needed that dress' (opinion).)

Here's how you keep them straight. A *fact* is a statement that can be proven to be true. An *opinion* is a statement that is a personal point of view or judgement. Verbs such as *is*, *show*, *confirm* and *demonstrate* can sometimes act as signal words to indicate a fact — for example, 'The Earth is a planet'. Verbs such as *love*, *like*, *claim* and *think* can sometimes act as signal words to indicate an opinion — for example, 'I like vanilla ice-cream'.

Adjectives that add real information act as signal words to indicate a fact — for example, 'Three black kittens were in the basket'. Adjectives such as *funny*, *awesome* and *boring*, and adverbs such as *really*, *much* and *worse* can act as signal words to indicate an opinion — for example, 'Watching the kittens tumble out of the basket was really funny'.

Looking for context clues

Using *context clues*, or signals within words, sentences and paragraphs, is another way to increase your understanding of texts. Sometimes you can even use context clues within words to help with word meanings. Word parts such as prefixes and suffixes are clues to the meaning of a word. For example, the suffix *-ible* means 'able to be' or 'capable of'.

A *prefix* is a word part added to the beginning of a word to create a new word. Adding a prefix does not change the spelling of the base word. A *suffix* is a word part added to the end of a word to create a new word. Suffixes often change the spelling of the word they're added to. (See Chapter 13 for more information.)

Greek and Latin roots can also give context clues to help with word meanings — for example, knowing that the word root *audio* means 'hear' can help you understand the meaning of the word *audible*. (Also see Chapter 13 for more information on the Greek and Latin roots of words.)

You can also use context clues from the sentence structure or from *figurative language*. Or you can read around a word — the clue to a word's meaning can sometimes be found in other parts of the sentence, where a difficult word is restated in simpler language. Sometimes the meaning of a word can be guessed because a signal word or phrase in the sentence precedes another word that has a similar or opposite meaning.

Usage troubleshooting guide

Some words just seem to love getting in the way — popping up when really another word is ready and able, and much better suited to the task. Using them can also cause your word processor grammar checker to hand out the squiggly lines.

You can use the following to keep these (sometimes troublesome) words in their place:

✔ **between** or **among**: Use *between* for two and *among* for more than two. For example:

Geoff and Maria divided the proceeds of the garage sale **between** them.

The last of the water was divided **among** the four hikers.

✔ **best** or **better**: If you are comparing two things, you say one is *better* than the other. If you are comparing more than two things, you say that one is *best*. For example:

Our team proved itself the **better** side on the day.

Michael Jackson was considered by his fans the **best** singer in the world.

✔ **between you and I/between you and me**: *Between* is a preposition and must be

followed in the sentence by *me*. Similarly, *between him and her* is correct, and *between he and she* is incorrect.

✔ **can** or **may**: *Can* means to be able to, while *may* means to be allowed or to be permitted. For example:

Once you **can** swim, the beach becomes a safer place.

You **may** watch TV after you have finished your homework.

✔ **fewer** or **less**: Use *fewer* for number (things that can be counted individually) and *less* for quantity (things that can't be counted). For example:

There were **fewer** than thirty people at the party.

We have had **less** rain this year than last year.

✔ **good** or **well**: *Good* is an adjective and *well* is an adverb. So saying, 'She did **good** at the athletics meet' is incorrect because good (an adjective) is being used as an adverb. Correct usage is:

She did **well** at the athletics meet.

✔ **loan** or **lend**: Both *lend* and *loan* can be used as verbs, but only loan should be used as a noun, and not lend. So 'Pieta gave me a **lend** of ten dollars' is incorrect. The correct usage is:

Pieta gave me a **loan** of ten dollars.

✔ **that/which/who**: Use *who* for people, and *which* or *that* for things. For example:

Juanita is the girl **who** was elected as class captain.

Katrina's car, **which** she loved, was a write-off.

The strawberries **that** we picked were sweet and tasty.

✔ **should have/could have/would have**: In speech or writing you may contract these to *should've, could've, would've*. In each contraction the *'ve* takes the place of *have*. Never write them as *should of, could of, would of*.

✔ **try and/try to**: *Try and* is used in casual speech. In writing it should be edited as:

Try to come to my party on Saturday.

✔ **who** or **whom**: These days the rule about the usage of *whom* isn't as strictly applied as it was in the past. In informal writing, you probably don't need to worry about it so much. For formal writing, however, you're still best to follow the correct usage. Some examples of usage of *who* and *whom* are:

This is the boy **who** threw the ball. (*Who* must be used in this sentence because it is the subject of the verb *threw*.)

This is the boy **whom** the teacher asked to collect the books.

This is the boy **who** the teacher asked to collect the books.

(Because *whom* is the object of the verb *is*, *whom* was traditionally considered correct in the preceding example. However, both are considered acceptable today when used as the object of a clause.) *Whom* should always be used after a preposition. For example:

Mandy was the person to **whom** I gave the extra ticket.

Considering Connections within Texts

The previous few sections in this chapter focus on ways to increase your understanding as you read text — that is, to improve your reading comprehension. Some final ways to improve understanding are looking at cause and effect, and comparing and contrasting.

In texts, one event may result in another event: this is *cause and effect*. When the text describes events in order, or sequence, the cause comes before the effect. When the text describes events out of sequence or order, the cause may be found after the effect.

Signal words such as *because, since, so, as a result, consequently* and *therefore* can help you recognise cause and effect.

Finding *comparing and contrasting* ideas also helps you comprehend what you read and formulate your ideas about it. A *comparison* states how two things are similar. A *contrast* states how two things are different.

Signal words for comparison include *by comparison, equally, in the same way, similarly, likewise* and *just as*. Signal words for contrast include *conversely, but, despite, however, instead, nevertheless, rather than, on the other hand* and *on the contrary*.

Chapter 13

Blitzing the Spelling Bee

. . . .

In This Chapter

▷ Working out how words are formed

▷ Gaining confidence with some spelling rules and tricks

▷ Understanding how vowel and consonant sounds are spelled

▷ Spelling the endings of words correctly

. . . .

Spelling is the way we all form written words, using letters in an accepted order. All words in the English language are spelled using a combination of one or more of the five vowel letters (a, e, i, o, u) and the 21 consonant letters of the alphabet.

In this chapter, we take you through some of the basic (and not so basic) tricks to spelling. Soon you'll be teaching your spell checker a thing or two!

Understanding the Basics of Spelling

Your spelling and vocabulary can be improved if you know about and understand the following:

✔ Word families that are formed from base words

✔ Word origins such as Greek and Latin roots and prefixes and suffixes

✔ Spelling of singular and plural forms of words

✔ Silent letters

✔ Regular spellings that follow rules

✔ Irregular spellings that do not follow rules

The following sections take you through these concepts.

Keeping it together: Word families

Word families are groups of words that have a common base word. Prefixes and suffixes can be added to the base word to create a range of new words.

A *base word* is the simplest form of a word. These brave words can stand alone and can't be reduced to a shorter word. Base words are friendly fellows, though, and new words can be formed with them. For example, *run* is a base word from which you can form other words such as *running*, *re-run* and *runner*. Understanding about base words can help with the spelling and meaning of words.

Have a look at the base word *happy*. From this, you can form happiness, unhappy, unhappiness, happier, happiest. You create this range of new words by adding prefixes and suffixes (see the section 'Spotting a prefix and a suffix', later in this chapter, for more).

A suffix will often tell you what part of speech or word class (refer to Chapter 1) the new word is. The suffixes *ness* and *ment*, for example, tell you the word is a noun.

Working out Greek and Latin word roots

Many words in the English language have Greek and Latin roots. A *word root* contains the core meaning of a word but can't always stand on its own. Knowing common word roots can help you with the meaning and spelling of many words.

Greek word roots include *graph*, meaning 'write', and *bios*, meaning 'life'. From these, the English words *paragraph* and *biology* are formed. Latin word roots include *audio*, meaning 'hear', and *annus*, meaning 'year'. From these, the English words *audience* and *anniversary* are formed.

Table 13-1 provides some Greek roots and the English words that have come from them, while Table 13-2 provides the same for Latin roots.

Table 13-1	Greek Roots and English Examples	
Root	*Meaning*	*Examples*
astera	star	astronomy, astronaut
bios	life	biography, biology

Root	Meaning	Examples
chronos	time	chronology, synchronise
demos	the people	democracy, epidemic
ge	the earth	geography, geology
grapho	I write	autograph, paragraph
logos	a word, a speech, or a stud	dialogue, catalogue
mikros	small	microscope, microbe
phone	sound	telephone, microphone
skopeo	I view	telescope, periscope
tele	far	telephone, telegraph

Table 13-2	Latin Roots and English Examples	
Root	**Meaning**	**Examples**
aequus	equal, fair, just	equivalent, equilateral
annus	a year	anniversary, annuity
audio	I hear	audience, auditorium
cado	I fall	accident, deciduous
cedo	I go	succeed, antecedent
centum	a hundred	century, centipede
corpus	the body	corpse, incorporate
credo	I believe	credible, credential
decem	ten	decimal, decimate
dico	I say	diction, verdict
finis	the end	define, finalist
frango	I break	fraction, fragile
gradus	step	gradual, degree
jungo	I join	conjunction, joint
lego	I read, I choose	elect, legible

(continued)

Table 13-2 *(continued)*

Root	Meaning	Examples
loquor	I speak	loquacious, soliloquy
magnus	great	magnify, magnificent
manus	the hand	manufacture, manual
mater	mother	maternal, matron
mitto	I send	transmit, remit
modus	a manner, a measure	mode, modern
novus	new	novelty, innovate
pars	part	particle, participate
pater	father	paternal, patriarch
pax	peace	pact, pacify
pello	I drive	propel, compulsion
pono	place	preposition, deposit
porto	I carry	portable, transport
scribe	I write	prescribe, describe
solus	alone	solitary, desolate
specio	I see	spectator, suspect
spiro	I breathe	respiration, perspire
tango	I touch	contagious, contact
unus	one	unanimous, union
vivo	I live	survive, vital
Volvo	I roll	involve, revolt

Spotting a prefix and a suffix

A *prefix* is a word part added to the beginning of a word to create a new word. For example, adding the prefix *pre* before the base word *view* creates a new word: *preview*. Adding the prefix *un* before the base word *happy* results in a word with the opposite meaning. Adding a prefix does not change the spelling of the base word.

A *suffix* is a word part added to the end of a word to create a new word. Suffixes can be added to base words or longer words. Suffixes can also tell you what class or part of speech a word is: noun, verb, adjective or adverb. By adding suffixes, you can make nouns (such as 'informant'), adjectives (such as 'wooden'), adverbs (such as 'sadly') and verbs (such as 'activate').

Suffixes often change the spelling of the word they're added to. For example, *hungry* + *ly* becomes 'hungrily'.

Solo or a group: Singular and plural forms

Here we can start out pretty simply. The *singular* form of a noun is used when referring to a single person or thing. The *plural* form is used for more than one person or thing. (Easy, right?) You even have some rules that govern how most plurals are formed. For example, to form the plural of a noun such as *boy*, *rock* or *dish*, you add *-s* or *-es* — to create *boys*, *rocks*, *dishes*.

But then you have to get a bit trickier. Some plural forms are *irregular* and must be learned — for example, *mouse* becomes *mice* and *woman* becomes *women*. Some words have the same singular and plural form — for example, *sheep*, *deer*, *series* and *species*.

The following provides some help dealing with stickier plural forms:

- ✔ **Singular words ending in *s*, *sh*, *tch*, *x* and *z*:** These have *es* added to them to form the plural. For example, *dress* becomes *dresses*, *watch* becomes *watches*, *waltz* becomes *waltzes*, *wish* becomes *wishes* and *box* becomes *boxes*.

- ✔ **Singular words ending in *ch*:** These usually have *es* added to them to form the plural. However, if the *ch* is pronounced *k*, the plural is formed with just *s*. For example, *church* becomes *churches* and *monarch* becomes *monarchs*.

- ✔ **Singular words that end in *y*:** These normally have *s* added to them to form the plural — for example, *toy* becomes *toys*. If a consonant appears before the *y*, however, the *y* changes to an *i* before adding *es* — for example, *hobby* becomes *hobbies*.

- ✔ **Some singular words ending in *f* and *fe*:** These drop the ending and add *ves* to form the plural — *leaf* becomes *leaves* and *knife* becomes *knives*.

Some plural forms of words just don't follow the rules at all! Table 13-3 shows plural forms, including some irregular forms.

Table 13-3	Plural Forms of Words
Singular	*Plural*
analysis	analyses
antithesis	antitheses
apex	apexes/apices
appendix	appendixes/appendices
axis	axes
bacterium	bacteria
basis	bases
bonus	bonuses
cactus	cacti
cargo	cargoes
crisis	crises
criterion	criteria
curriculum	curricula/curriculums
datum	data
dwarf	dwarfs/dwarves
echo	echoes
elf	elves
erratum	errata
fish	fish/fishes
formula	formulae
fungus	fungi
gas	gases
genre	genres
hero	heroes
hippopotamus	hippopotamuses/hippopotami
hoof	hoofs/hooves
index	indexes/indices
larva	larvae
matrix	matrices/matrixes

Singular	Plural
maximum	maximums/maxima
medium	media
menu	menus
minimum	minimums/minima
mosquito	mosquitoes
mother-in-law	mothers-in-law
motto	mottos/mottoes
nucleus	nuclei
oasis	oases
octopus	octopuses
phenomenon	phenomena
photo	photos
piano	pianos
platypus	platypuses
plus	pluses
potato	potatoes
quiz	quizzes
quota	quotas
radius	radii
referendum	referendums/referenda
rhinoceros	rhinoceroses/rhinoceros
roof	roofs
salmon	salmon
scenario	scenarios
series	series
shampoo	shampoos
ski	skis
species	species
stimulus	stimuli
syllabus	syllabuses/syllabi

(continued)

Table 13-3 *(continued)*

Singular	Plural
taxi	taxis
tomato	tomatoes
tornado	tornadoes
virus	viruses
volcano	volcanoes
wharf	wharves/wharfs
zero	zeros/zeroes

Silencing silent letters

Silent letters are letters that are included in the written word but are not sounded when the word is spoken. The letters *b, g, gh, h, k, l, n, p, s, t* and *w* can sometimes be silent. For example, *b* is sometimes silent after *m* (comb), *w* is silent before *r* (wrap) and is sometimes silent before *h* (who). In the words *knight* and *know*, the *k* is silent.

Staying regular (and irregular)

Regular spellings are words that play along and follow spelling rules. These words are unlikely to cause you much stress (and they certainly won't stay out too late at night.) You can simply remember some common rules and use these as a guide when spelling the words that follow the rules — which includes many English words. For example, one rule is, 'Use *i* before *e* except after *c*'. Words that follow this rule include *believe, field, piece, receive* and *ceiling*. (See the section, 'Applying spelling rules and tips', later in this chapter, for more.)

Irregular spellings are words that are exceptions to spelling rules (they're the rebels hanging out at the back of the class). These words must be learned through use.

Just to try to trip you up even more, some words have alternative spellings called *variants*. Some, such as *finalise* or *finalize*, are considered equally acceptable. Others, such as *color*, are less widely accepted in Australia. (*Colour* is usual here — see the section 'Applying spelling rules and tips', later in this chapter, for more.) And some words come from other languages and so they don't follow English spelling rules, such as *pizza*.

Some words are considered spelling 'demons', and these are commonly misspelled — examples include *rhythm*, *picnicker* and *vacuum*. (See the sidebar 'Facing your spelling demons' for a whole lot more.)

Taking Advantage of Spelling Strategies

One way to learn how to spell tricky words is to apply some spelling tricks or strategies that work for you. You can learn to use memory aids, for example, such as seeing letter patterns or using sound cues such as rhymes. Try these out:

> hear, here ... I hear with my ear.

> separate ... I smell a rat in separate.

Here's a sure-fire strategy for learning how to spell any word:

- ✔ **Look** at the word, separating it into syllables to see how it is constructed — for example, vertebrate splits into *ver-te-brate* (see the following section for more on this).
- ✔ **Say** the word to hear how it sounds.
- ✔ **Write** the word, so that you are making a conscious effort to match letters and sounds.
- ✔ **Use** the word so that it becomes familiar.

A similar strategy is **Look, Say, Cover, Write, Check**. (If you're feeling extra creative, you can even make up a rhyme for this strategy.)

The following sections take you through some further spelling strategies.

Being syllable savvy

Breaking words into syllables is a good way to learn their spelling. A *syllable* is a part of a word. It contains a vowel sound and may contain consonant sounds around the vowel.

Here are some examples of words with different numbers of syllables:

- ✔ **One syllable:** go
- ✔ **Two syllables:** nervous (ner-vous)

✔ **Three syllables:** elephant (el-e-phant)

✔ **Four syllables:** impatiently (im-pa-tient-ly)

✔ **Five syllables:** imperiously (im-per-i-ous-ly)

Applying spelling rules and tips

Here are some rules and tips to help you deal with spelling challenges:

✔ **Use *i* before *e* except after *c*:** For example, *believe*, *field*, *piece*, *achieve*, *receive*, *deceive* and *ceiling*. While exceptions do exist — such as foreign, seize and weird — the rule does hold in most cases where the sound is *ee* as in *see*.

✔ **When *y* is at the start of a word, it acts like a consonant:** This works for *yard* and *yell*.

✔ **When *y* is at the end of a word, or has an *i* sound, it acts as a vowel:** For example, *valley* and *gym*.

✔ **Words ending in *our* can also be spelt with *or*.** This includes *colour*, *honour* and *vigour*.

In Australia, the most common spelling is with *our* but some magazines and newspapers use the variant *or*. Whichever spelling variant you choose, make sure you're consistent throughout your writing.

✔ **Some words ending in *ise* can also be spelt with *ize*.** In Australia, the more common usage is *ise* — for example, *organise* rather than *organize*.

✔ **For words ending in a single consonant, double that last letter before adding endings beginning with a vowel:** For example *sad* becomes *sadder* and *saddest*; *thin* becomes *thinner* and *thinnest*; *clap* becomes *clapped* and *clapping*.

Do not double the final consonant of a one-syllable word if the word ends with two or more consonants — for example, *faster* and *debtor*.

✔ **For words where the vowel is spelt with two letters, do not double the final consonant:** For example, *sweet* becomes *sweeter* or *sweetest*, and *soak* becomes *soaked* and *soaking*.

✔ **For two-syllable words, double the last consonant if the second syllable is stressed:** For example, *begin* becomes *beginning*.

Do not double the final consonant if the word has a strong stress on the first syllable — for example *offer* becomes *offering* and *offered*

Whether to double the final *l* in a word like *equal* (*equalled* or *equaled*) or *medal* (*medallist* and *medalist*) is a point of discussion. (Although your spell checker may have a few ideas.) In Australian spelling, the double *ll* is commonly used. ***Note:*** The *l* is never doubled before *ise* — for example, *formalise* and *legalise*.

✔ **For some words ending in *c*, add a *k* before an ending:** For example, *picnic* and *panic* become *picnicker* and *panicked*. This avoids the confusion of thinking the *c* has an *s* sound (as it does in many other words).

Handling hard and soft sounds

Just to mix things up a bit, the letters *c* and *g* can be pronounced in different ways. The letter *c* can have a 'hard' sound, as in *car*, *cot* and *custard*; or it can have a 'soft' sound, as in *circle* and *cylinder*. The letter *g* can have a hard sound, as in *gasp* and *goose*; or it can have a soft sound, as in *gym* and *ginger*.

How do you know when the soft *g* sound is spelled with the letter *g* or the letter *j* or even *dg*? Well, we can give you some help. The letter *j* is almost always used if the sound is followed by an *a*, *o* or *u*: *jog*, *just*, *jar*. The letter *g* is often used to spell the soft *g* sound when it is followed by an *e*, *i* or *y*: *ginger*, *gentle*, *gem*, *aged*, *algebra*, *origin*, *gym*. There are exceptions (of course!), such as *jelly*, *jetty*, *jest*, *jinx* and *jig*. But if the soft *g* sound comes immediately after a short vowel sound, it is usually spelled *dg*. For example: *judge*, *badge*, *hedge*.

Getting around tricky sounds

If you can't easily find the word you're looking up (in a dictionary or spelling guide), it might be that the word begins with a letter or letters that you say in a different way to normal or which may be completely silent. Table 13-4 can help you track down those tricky words.

Table 13-4	Words with Tricky Sounds	
Sound that the Word Begins With	*The Word Could Begin with This*	*Example*
ch	c	cello
f	ph	photo
g	gh	ghost
g	gu	guide
h	wh	whole
j	g	gem
k	ch	character
k	qu	quiche
k	kh	khaki
kw	qu	quite
n	gn	gnash
n	kn	knee
n	pn	pneumonia
r	rh	rhyme
r	wr	write
s	c	cereal
s	ps	psychology
s	sc	science
s	sw	sword
sh	s	sugar
sh	sch	schedule
sh	ch	champagne
sk	sch	school
t	th	thyme
t	tw	two
w	wh	white
z	x	xylophone

Facing your spelling demons

Spelling demons are those words you are most likely to misspell. Some of these words are listed here, and a great way to become a superior speller is to learn these by heart.

But you can also compile your own list of personal spelling demons and add them to the ones we've provided.

accessible	deceive	knowledge	receive
accommodate	definitely	language	recognise
advertisement	description	leisure	reluctant
announcement	disappointed	length	rhyme
Antarctic	equipped	liaison	rhythm
antique	exaggerate	lizard	secluded
athletes	excitement	loneliness	sensitive
atmosphere	explanation	longitude	separate
awkward	fatigued	marathon	shriek
balance	finally	martyr	since
beginning	fitness	mischief	stomach
believe	government	mischievous	substantial
burglar	grateful	narrative	success
claws	height	nuisance	surgery
climb	heirloom	overnight	taste
colloquial	hiding	overwhelmed	thought
committee	immediately	particles	vacuum
community	immigrant	peaceful	variety
consumed	impossible	performance	vehicle
convenience	indigenous	poisonous	version
cupboard	intelligence	previously	woollen
dangerous	kilojoule	psychiatrist	

Using Vowel and Consonant Sounds

Sometimes you can pay attention to the vowel and consonant sounds within words to gain some clues to how they might be spelled. For example, vowel sounds within words can be spelled in a number of ways, and sounds can be short or long.

The following lists some common vowel sounds and how they might be spelled:

- ✔ **Words using the vowel sounds _a_, _ay_ and _ah_:** The short sound _a_ (as in _cat_) is almost always spelled with an 'a' — for example, _pack_, _astronaut_. The long sound _ay_ (as in _mate_) can be spelled in a number of ways — for example, _pain_, _crayon_, _break_, _eight_, _grey_. The long sound _ah_ (as in _vase_) can be spelled in a number of ways, such as _grass_, _laugh_, _part_, _half_.

- ✔ **Words using the vowel sounds _aw_ and _air_:** The long sound _aw_ (as in _yawn_) can be spelled in a number of ways — for example, _law_, _talk_, _roar_, _bore_, _bought_, _caught_, _door_, _sure_. The long sound _air_ (as in _hair_) can be spelled in a number of ways, such as _chair_, _share_, _pear_, _there_, _their_.

- ✔ **Words using the vowel sounds _e_, _ee_, _er_ and _ear_:** The short vowel sound _e_ (as in _bell_) can be spelled in a number of ways — for example, _red_, _bread_, _friend_, _bury_. The long sound _ee_ (as in _see_) can be spelled in a number of ways — _demon_, _flea_, _teen_, _ceiling_, _key_, _sardine_, _field_. The long sound _er_ (as in _perk_) can be spelled in a number of ways — _learn_, _service_, _bird_, _work_, _journey_, _purse_. The long sound _ear_ (as in _appear_) can be spelled in a number of ways — _fear_, _beer_, _here_, _pier_.

- ✔ **Words using the vowel sounds _i_ and _ie_:** The short vowel sound _i_ (as in _hit_) can be spelled in a number of ways — _bin_, _build_, _pyramid_. The long vowel sound _ie_ (as in _drive_) can be spelled in a number of ways — _tied_, _lime_, _sight_, _goodbye_, _fly_.

- ✔ **Words using the vowel sounds _o_, _oh_, _ow_ and _oy_:** The short vowel sound _o_ (as in _drop_) can be spelled in a number of ways — _wasp_, _sausage_, _plot_, _cough_. The long sound _oh_ (as in _joke_) can be spelled in a number of ways — _phone_, _soap_, _toe_, _flow_. The long sound _ow_ (as in _clown_) can be spelled in a number of ways — _loud_, _frown_, _bough_. The long sound _oy_ (as in _toy_) can be spelled in a number of ways — _coin_, _boy_, _buoy_.

- ✔ **Words using the vowel sounds _u_, _oo_, _ooh_ and _yew_:** The short vowel sound _u_ (as in _luck_) can be spelled in a number of ways — _come_, _touch_, _much_. The short sound _oo_ (as in _book_) can be spelled in a number of ways — _look_, _could_, _full_. The long sound _ooh_ (as in _rude_) can be spelled in a number of ways — _flew_, _do_, _boot_, _soup_, _flute_, _fruit_. The long sound _yew_ (as in _use_) can be spelled in a number of ways — _new_, _duty_, _imbue_, _view_.

Consonant sounds within words can also give clues to how they might be spelled, as follows:

- **Words using the consonant sounds *f*, *g* and *j*:** The sound *f* (as in *funny*) can be spelled in a number of ways— *photo, giraffe, half, laugh*. The sound *g* (as in *game*) can be spelled in a number of ways — *glad, ghost, egg, guide*. The sound *j* (as in *jump*) can be spelled in a number of ways — *gem, fudge, jail*.

- **Words using the consonants *k* and *s*:** The sound *k* (as in *kick*) can be spelled in a number of ways — *cat, accommodate, character, luck, quiche, khaki*. The sound *s* (as in *sister*) can be spelled in a number of ways — *summer, scent, missing*.

- **Words using the consonant sounds *sh*, *z* and *ch*:** The sound *sh* (as in *shoe*) can be spelled in a number of ways — *champagne, special, sugar, dimension, mission, combination*. The sound *z* (as in *zoo*) can be spelled in a number of ways— *fizzy, cheese, dessert, xylophone*. The sound *ch* (as in *check*) can be spelled in a number of ways — *cello, catch, righteous, question, nature*.

Knowing the Correct Endings

As covered earlier in this chapter, a *suffix* is a word part that is added to the end of a base word. No clear rule tells you which suffix to use (well, what did you expect?); however, some generalisations apply that can help you select the appropriate suffix.

These generalisations can be applied as follows:

- **Choosing *-ous*, *-ious* or *-eous*:** The word endings *-ous*, *-ious* and *-eous* are suffixes that form adjectives. If the base word ends in a consonant, simply add *-ous* — for example, *dangerous*. If a word ends in a silent *e*, simply drop the 'e' and add *-ous* — *adventurous*. If a word ends in a soft *c* or *g*, keep the 'e' before *-ous*. This keeps the soft sound of the base word — for example, *courageous*. If a word ends in a *y*, drop the 'y' and add either *-eous* or *-ious* — *furious, plenteous*.

  The *-ious* ending is much more common than the *-eous* ending.

- **Choosing between *-able* and *-ible*:** The word endings *-able* and *-ible* are suffixes that form adjectives. If the base word is written in full, the most usual ending is *-able* — for example, *respectable*, where the base word, *respect*, is written in full. When only part of the base word is used, the word ending is *-ible* — for example, *horrible*.

Some words that are made up of complete base words still take the ending *-ible*. Learning these words is a good idea — an example is *convertible*.

✔ **Choosing between *-ance* and *-ence*:** The word endings *-ance* and *-ence* are suffixes that form nouns. Add *-ance* when the base word ends with a hard *c* or a hard *g* — for example, *elegance*. Also add *-ance* when the base word ends with *-ear* — *appearance*. Add *-ance* when the base word ends with *-ure* — for example, *endurance*. However, add *-ence* when the base word ends with a soft *c* or a soft *g* — for example, *innocence*. Also add *-ence* when the base word ends in *-ist* — *existence*.

Part IV
The Part of Tens

the
part of
tens

In this part . . .

- ✔ Understand how to correct, and avoid, common grammar errors.

- ✔ Work out the ways you're better than the grammar checker on your computer.

- ✔ Improve the quality of your writing with some quick tips.

Chapter 14

Ten Solutions to the Most Common Grammar Errors

. . . .

In This Chapter

▶ Placing apostrophes perfectly

▶ Using verbs with confidence

▶ Completing sentences correctly

. . . .

*N*obody's perfect. We all make mistakes and, quite honestly, the English language is so tricky that tripping up is easy. So, in this chapter, we look at ten common grammar hiccups — the sort that inspire your grammar checker to decorate your documents with wiggly green lines and helpfully suggest that you consider revising your words. Here, we take the next step and show you how to make those revisions.

Adding Apostrophes (Or Not)

If apostrophes were people, they'd all need regular counselling. They're the most misunderstood and abused of all punctuation marks. You can help rebuild their self-esteem by remembering that *it's* means *it is* or *it has* in the same way that *she's* means *she is* or *she has*, and *he's* means *he is* or *he has*. Under no circumstances and in no instance does *it's* ever mean belonging to it. *Its* without the apostrophe means belonging to it. Always. In every case. No exception with that one. You'd never put an apostrophe in *his*, *hers* or *ours* (meaning belonging to him, her or us), so don't put one in *its* — unless you mean *it is* or *it has*.

The second most common apostrophe catastrophe involves confusion about where to put the little wiggle when the word you want to turn into a possessive ends in the letter *s*. (A *possessive* is, of course, a word that shows ownership.) The solution is simple. Apply the always rules and you can't be wrong. Always add apostrophe + *s* when the word you want to turn into a possessive is singular (one thing). Yes, that's right, always — even if the word ends in *s*, as in *Jess's frown* or *cactus's spike*. It may look odd, but it isn't wrong. And always add the apostrophe after the *s* if the word is plural (more than one thing). Again, *the Joneses' contribution* might look weird, but if the contribution was made by all of the Joneses, the apostrophe is in the right place. (Chapter 8 deals with apostrophes.)

Reaching Agreement

The rule is simple. All verbs must match up with their subjects (the *who* or *what* performing the verb); all pronouns must match up with their antecedents (the word the pronoun stands in for). That's what this kind of agreement is; everybody in the Land of Sentence pairs up agreeably with the appropriate partner. Nobody is left standing alone in a corner and, most certainly, nobody tries to match up with somebody else's partner.

Thus, if the subject is singular (just one), so are the verb and the pronoun: *The author lost her mind*. And if the subject is plural (more than one), so are the verb and the pronoun: *Authors lose their minds*.

When the whole thing gets murky is when the subject looks singular but means something plural, or vice versa. We say *The staff wants improved conditions* (singular) because even though lots of staff members are in the company, they're acting as one united body. We say *The staff want to bring their partners to the function* (plural) because the staff is acting as individuals: presumably they don't all share one partner. To help decide in such cases, try putting the words *The whole* (staff, team, committee or whatever) in front of the verb. If your sentence makes sense that way, you need a singular verb. (Chapters 2 and 4 cover agreement.)

Staying in the Right Tense

Okay, listen up. Illegally switching tenses within a piece of writing is a common problem that can prove fatal. You must avoid unauthorised movement between past, present and future tense. To be clear about that: verbs have three main tenses. In the *past tense* something happened. In the *present tense*, something happens. In the *future tense*, something will happen. Sometimes, jumping from one tense to the other is necessary to put your communication in the correct time frame but, mostly, whatever you're writing should stay with just one tense.

Two tricks could help you with this. You can keep looking back at the verbs you've chosen earlier in the document to remind you what tense you should be using. Alternatively, picture what you're writing about as events marked on a time line with the central point being 'now — present tense'. That should help you decide which tense is needed. (Chapters 2 and 3 have more information about verbs than you could poke a stick at.)

Splicing Sentences with a Comma

When you splice two pieces of rope together, you twist the frayed ends into one and hope the join will hold. When you splice two complete, independent ideas together with a comma, you create a join that cannot hold. We call this error a *comma splice*.

The comma is a weakling that never learned how to tie a double fisherman's knot. If you want to join two complete ideas, use a conjunction (joining word) or a punctuation mark with holding power: a semicolon. Complete ideas joined with a semicolon look like this: *Nicole loves to sing; Joel hates to listen*. Joined with a conjunction, they would be something like *Nicole loves to sing but Joel hates to listen*. (Conjunctions crop up in Chapter 4, while Chapter 7 handles the correct use of commas and semicolons.)

Running Sentences On

The comma splice (refer to preceding section) has a sibling: the *run-on sentence*. This problem child comes to visit when you make no attempt to create a join or link between complete ideas, but instead simply dump them, nose-to-tail, in one sentence. You can eliminate this monster in exactly the same ways that you banish a comma splice, with a conjunction or a semicolon. Have a look at the example in the preceding section for information about how to use semicolons or conjunctions to be rid of this pest. The solution is the same. (Chapter 7 shows you the correct way to join ideas with punctuation marks: the colon and its relative the semicolon hold the key.)

Fragmenting Sentences

A meaningful group of words that begins with a capital letter and ends with a full stop is not necessarily a sentence. To qualify as a fully certified sentence, the group of words must contain a matching subject–verb pair. Without that pair, what you have is not a sentence but a sentence fragment.

Over the bridge, past the station and towards her favourite bookshop is a sentence fragment. Who did what in that sentence? We don't know. So, to revise it into a legitimate sentence, we must add a matching subject–verb pair. *Charlotte saunters over the bridge, past the station and towards her favourite bookshop.* Now we have a sentence. (Chapter 4 gets down to the nitty-gritty of complete sentences and fragments.)

Misplacing Modifiers

Putting a modifier in the wrong place is like hanging a magnificent piece of art over a window or opposite a crooked mirror. The artwork loses its impact in the confusion of too much glare or a distorted reflection. Misplaced modifiers are descriptions that have been put in the wrong place, like this: *Lucinda was walking the dog in her new stilettos.* While it's altogether possible that Lucinda has a female dog, and that Lucinda would humiliate the poor thing by making it wear shoes, it's highly unlikely that the dog could manage stilettos. So, to revise a sentence that contains a misplaced modifier, move the description closer to the word/s it's modifying, like this: *Lucinda, in her new stilettos, was walking the dog.* (Chapter 6 talks more about modifying with adjectives and adverbs.)

Knowing When to Use Subject and Object Pronouns

The subject pronouns are *I, you, he, she, it, we* and *they*. The object pronouns are *me, you, him, her, it, us* and *them*. This may sound obvious, but you should choose a subject pronoun when a pronoun is the subject of the verb in your sentence (remember that you find the subject by asking the question '*Who* or *what* is performing or being the verb?'). Choose an object pronoun for everything else. (If this tip isn't obvious enough for you, Chapter 4 can set you straight.)

Selecting Prepositions

Prepositions are words that go in front of nouns and show a relationship in time or space (*under* the counter, *over* the top). Of all the tens of thousands of words in the English language, fewer than 200 of them are prepositions. And yet, three of those little words make it into the Top Ten Most Used Words in English (no, not 'I love you'— none of those words are prepositions). Those three little words are — *of, in* and *to.*

No rules really exist about how to choose the right preposition — you're just supposed to know which one goes where by language osmosis. Your dictionary is the place to find the help you may need. Look carefully at prepositions when you're editing your work. They can be very troublesome.

Here are a few examples so that you know what you're looking for

This sentence has an extra preposition (shown with the strikethrough): *Tom's sunglasses fell off ~~of~~ the dashboard.*

This sentence contains the wrong preposition (with the correct one shown in round brackets): *I'm bored ~~of~~ (with) this.*

So does this one: *She's angry ~~at~~ (with) me.* And this one is missing the preposition *on*: *They went to the movie (on) Sunday afternoon.*

And here are a few solutions to common preposition problems that tend to trip people up:

- ✔ In Australia, it is best to use *different from* — not *different than* or *different to.*

- ✔ *Beside* means positioned next to. *Besides* means as well, or moreover. It is a joining word, not a preposition.

- ✔ In general, *between* is used when you're taking about two things. *Among* is used for larger groups.

- ✔ You do something either *on* purpose or *by* accident.

Confusing 'Of' with 'Have'

Aussies are famous for effortlessly turning most vowel sounds into a multi-purpose grunt. When we abbreviate *would have* to *would've*, the word that comes out of our mouths sounds like *would of.* So that's what people write, which is incorrect. Solution: Don't do it!

Chapter 15

Ten Things Grammar and Spell Checkers Can't Do

*V*ery few writers manage to create squiggle-free documents. Squiggly lines warn you of possible errors as you type. Some of your ooopses are likely even autocorrected without your noticing. Relying on your computer to detect your weaknesses, however, isn't wise. In this chapter we look at ten features of good writing that people can achieve, but spelling and grammar checkers can't.

Always Be Right

Unless you're one of those readers who starts at the back of the book, or always reads the shortest chapters first, by now you probably know that grammar is complicated. Your computer, as smart as it may seem, doesn't understand all the exceptions and exclusions and special cases that English grammar contains. Any computer is limited by the information that has been programmed into it, and applies that same information in all cases.

A grammar checker detects common errors by scanning your writing for particular patterns of words and punctuation marks. When it finds a certain pattern, a grammar checker alerts you to a possible problem. Sometimes, however, no problem exists. Even if you carefully set the preferences on your grammar checker to detect the errors that you know you make, coded language can never be as complex as written English. So, your grammar checker can't always be right. So now you can apply what you learn in this book to your writing and you'll be way ahead of your grammar checker.

Ask What You Meant

A joke that tickles the fancy of grammar-lovers the world over tells the story of an English professor who asked his students to punctuate the following sentence:

a woman without her man is nothing

His class came up with two completely different solutions to the task. All the male students wrote: A woman, without her man, is nothing. While the females of the class opted for: A woman: without her, man is nothing.

The moral of the story? Punctuation matters. Meaning and grammar are interlocked. The male students' sentence means that women are not important. The female version means the opposite. Of course, writers choose their words, but they also decide the order to put them in and the best way to punctuate them. All of those decisions help build meaning. Your grammar checker can't ask you what you meant to say. How could it tell which version of the professor's sentence you meant to write? It couldn't. But you could.

Make Decisions

By all means, use the spelling and grammar facilities in your computer. Use the thesaurus and the dictionary too. All of these are valuable tools and you'd have to be crazy to ignore them. Anything that supports you in creating clear, engaging documents is worthwhile.

Having potential errors highlighted and possible solutions presented for you to choose from is very helpful, but the computer can't decide which option is best. You have to do that. And you can't decide which word is right or which grammar option fits your needs if you don't understand the rules that form the basis for English grammar. Catch-22! See how helpful this book is? Keep it next to your computer for reference and it can help you make correct grammar choices whenever necessary. (This book is way smarter than a grammar checker.)

Detect Right Spelling but the Wrong Word

The spell checker is immensely helpful for detecting and correcting your typos. How many times have you keyed *teh* instead of *the*, or *adn* instead of *and*? A spell checker notices when you make these errors and others, such as doubling the wrong letter in a word like *parallel*. It picks up gremlins like *seperate* for *separate*, and fixes the problem if you forget one of the *m*'s in *accommodation*.

On the other hand, the spell checker can't warn you that you have just used *incontinence* instead of *inconvenience* in a letter of apology or *viscous* instead of *vicious* in a complaint email about the neighbour's dog. A spell checker will merrily accept *field* for *filed*, *prospective* for *perspective*, and *quite* for *quiet*. And it will often skip right over *your/you're*, *too/to/two* and *their/there/they're* (because the words are correctly spelled, even if they're not the words you meant to use). Your computer doesn't understand what you've written. It can locate a misspelled word, but can't recognise when you use the wrong word if it is correctly spelled. Proofread. Edit. Check. That's the only way to be sure your document contains only the words you intend.

Question Vague Pronoun Use

Correct grammar is not always the same as good grammar. According to the rules that your grammar checker knows, this sentence is fine:

> It says in today's paper that a storm is approaching.

All the words are in the right order and the sentence is complete. What's the problem? The problem is the very first word. *It*. To whom or what does that pronoun refer back? (A pronoun stands in as a substitute for a noun or noun group.) Well, nothing really. It's just hanging around being vague. The sentence should be something like: *I read in today's paper that a storm is approaching* or *The weather report in today's paper says a storm is approaching*. As far as the grammar checker is concerned, the sentence contains no errors, but you have logic. You can grasp subtle relationships between words.

Your grammar checker would be content with this sentence too:

> Portia told her partner that she was leaving.

Who's leaving? Portia or her partner? We don't know because the pronoun *she* can't decide whether to hang out with Portia, or with Portia's partner. Your astute editor's ear is offended by this messy sentence with its unclear pronoun, but your grammar checker couldn't care less about it. You know in this example you need to reword the sentence to avoid using pronouns, or make it clearer who the pronoun refers to — so you win again.

Know When Passive Voice Is Best

Your grammar checker is likely programmed to pounce gleefully on any sentence written in *passive* voice (where the subject receives the action of the verb). As soon as the grammar checker detects passive verb use, it nudges you and suggests that you think about revising the sentence into *active* voice (where the subject performs the action of the verb). It would likely ask you to change *A loaded gun was found at the scene* to *Constable Wright/Mildred/A passing stranger* (insert name of whoever happened upon the weapon) *found a loaded gun at the scene*. The active version focuses the attention on the person who found the gun; the passive version focuses on the gun itself.

In Chapter 3, we give four good reasons to choose the passive voice, but obviously grammar checkers haven't read that chapter yet.

Emphasise What Matters

A good writer arranges ideas into words and sentences with patterns that support the points they're making. Grammar checkers don't understand this. They don't choose descriptive words or decide which idea to put in the main part of a sentence. They don't even realise that some ideas are more important than others.

A grammar checker trumpets the presence of an incomplete sentence and tut-tuts at you to correct the grammar by adding whatever elements of the sentence may be missing. But what if you'd written half a sentence on purpose? Perhaps you decided to put a key idea in a short, blunt statement to draw attention to it.

Similarly, your grammar checker can become distressed if you write a very long sentence. And again, the length may be deliberate. It may be critical to your argument to put several points side by side in a single sentence. How would your computer know that? It may have some idea about what's technically correct, but it has no idea about how to stress what a reader needs to know.

Create Sentences That Flow

Applying the basic rules of grammar and ensuring that most words are spelled correctly certainly contributes to the accuracy and impact of an essay or a document, but it can't create rhythm and flow. That's only possible if you have feelings and a brain, and are able to hear the music of language. Grammar checkers don't have flair. (Chapters 11 and 12 look at how grammar and style work together to enhance what you write.)

Identify Plain English

Plain English documents can be understood at first reading. They communicate in clear, simple ways. Although your grammar checker advises you to restrict the length of sentences and write in active voice (with the subject performing the verb's action), it doesn't notice if you choose complicated words rather than everyday ones.

Grammar checkers may object if you string too many nouns together into something like *company employee–manager relations improvement program* or *overhead line worker safety protection procedures development*. This is helpful when you're preparing a plain language document. However, a grammar checker doesn't care if you say *in view of the fact that* when all you need is *because*, or refer to your mum's job as *the capacity in which she is employed*. That's not very helpful.

Replace a Careful Reader

No electronic editor can replace a careful reader (yet!). Written communication is complex. Good writing requires so much more than spelling accurately and following grammar rules. Words and patterns of words have subtle shades of meaning. Writers are people communicating with an audience of people. And people are infinitely more complicated than machines.

Chapter 16

Ten Ways to Improve Your Writing

In This Chapter

▶ Considering your reader

▶ Starting and finishing

▶ Improving your word choice and flow

▶ Creating rhythm and style in your writing

Sadly, even if you work your way through every valuable page in this book, you may still find yourself struck dumb when you look at a blank screen or piece of paper. So what's the point of all this good grammar and precise punctuation? Well, although it can't come up with ideas for you, good grammar creates no confusion for your audience when you communicate those ideas. Clear and accurate writing conveys the same (or as similar as possible) information to every reader. This book provides you with knowledge about some of the core skills of literacy and effective communication. It also helps you develop your skills as a critical reader and editor of your own essays and assignments.

In this chapter, we give you ten tricks to help you use your knowledge of how language works to get started on a piece of writing and to improve the overall quality and effectiveness of what you write.

Think about Your Reader

All writing has readers. If the audience for your writing is just one person, namely you, then it doesn't matter how you communicate (unless, of course, you scribble something out in such obscure and unique shorthand that even you can't decode it later). Otherwise, your writing is more effective and accurate if you have a real audience in mind. Thinking about the people at the other end of your writing helps you to decide what's relevant and valuable. If they're expert in the topic (like you), you'll choose different words and perhaps shorter explanations than if they have little or no previous knowledge of your topic. You may even put things in point form or as steps for a beginner. If you've been given specific guidelines, you'll need to consider these as you plan out your content.

So, before you begin to write, visualise your reader. Imagine your teacher or someone you know who is part of your target audience and write for him or her.

Make a Good First Impression

It's more than a cliché; it's a fact. First impressions count. How often have you made it to the end of a novel that had you snoring at the first paragraph, or a textbook chapter that took so long to reach the point that you forgot what it was meant to be about? The key is to get your reader's interest at the outset. Make sure you're clear about what it is you're about to write (an essay, a letter, an email, a short story) and who the audience will be, and then try completing these statements:

> What I want to say to my reader/s is … (Summarise your points in a sentence or two and make the main point your first communication.)
>
> What I want the reader/s to do after or while reading this is … (This is your purpose for writing, the reason for it. Even if the piece of writing is required for school assessment, knowing what response you're seeking from your reader helps you focus and avoid wasting anyone's time.)

Your first sentence should be an attention grabber. Short sentences often work as openers. You don't want to turn your reader off with a long, dull sentence. Think about what gets you involved, and then apply that thinking to your writing. You'll have your audience hanging on your every word.

Choose Strong Verbs

The words that create the movement and energy in your writing are the verbs. That's why they're sometimes known as 'doing words'. They should always be busy doing something valuable in a sentence. (Chapter 2 introduces you to the basics of verbs.)

It's better to *succeed* than to *do really well*. It's more forceful to *eliminate* a problem than to *get rid of* or *do away with* it. You can embroider and decorate a limp, lazy verb with as many other words as you like, but you won't turn it into a powerful verb. It'll just be a limp verb buried under tinsel. So choose strong verbs, not weaklings.

Choose Precise Words

Good writers choose words that have the right sound to contribute to the flow of a sentence. As we cover in Chapter 11, a thesaurus gives you alternatives to the words you've written (or are about to write), plus a range of similar words, and even opposites. The thesaurus can offer a word that both fits precisely because its meaning is perfect, and it improves the pattern and rhythm of what you've written. It may be just the right word because it creates an impact by repeating a letter or sound so the sentence rolls smoothly along the surface of the page. Or maybe you need a few crisp, short words to break up the flow of a sentence and draw attention to an idea. Strong verbs, specific nouns and colourful adjectives help your reader to see what you intend them to see and hear what you mean. (Refer to Chapters 11 and 12 for more help with descriptive writing and vocabulary.)

Just remember to choose words that sit comfortably with the rest of your piece. Selectively weed out any vague or weak words and then use a thesaurus to help you plant fresh ones. Your writing will improve and your vocabulary will grow.

Choose the Right Voice

If you're fully acquainted with Chapter 3, you'll know that verbs have a voice. (If not, you may need to flip back and introduce yourself to that topic.) Anyway, you can choose between two voices when you write — active and passive voice. In an active-voice sentence, the subject of the sentence is the performer or doer of the action of the verb. In passive voice, the opposite is true (opposite in grammar terms, that is). The subject of the sentence is having the verb performed to it.

You write a clear message. (Active-voice sentence.) Readers understand who is doing what. (Active sentence.) Most of your writing will and should be in active voice. Active voice is direct. It communicates clearly.

Your writing will be changed by passive voice. (Passive-voice sentence.) The doer of the action is omitted or pushed into the background by the choice of the passive voice. (Passive sentence.) So, choosing passive may make your writing sound wordy and uncomfortable.

Both voices have important uses. You need to use the one that best suits your purpose for writing.

Be Consistent

When you write, you make lots of choices. Sure, you choose the words and the order you put them in, but you have more choices than that. You have style choices. You decide whether to be formal or chatty; whether to ask questions or provide answers; whether to use full sentences, point form or numbered lists; whether to write *e-mail* or *email;* whether to use *generalise* or *generalize;* whether to use single (' ') or double (" ") quotation marks. Make consistent choices so that you communicate most clearly with your audience.

Be consistent about the style and tone of your document too. Don't switch between formal and casual tone, or present an illogical mixture of numbered points and whole paragraphs. If you have any doubts, choose a good Australian dictionary and a reputable grammar book (like this one!) and stick with what they say.

Stay on Track

Imagine you're in the middle of telling some guy at a party about something amazing that happened last week and you realise he's looking over your shoulder to see who else is in the room. So, you lose your train of thought (because you're now also having a conversation with yourself, inside your head, about what kind of person this guy really is) and the point of the great story you were telling becomes completely lost. You can lose your reader in the same way if you drift off-task when you're writing.

To ensure that you remain on track, ask yourself lots of questions as you write: *So what? What now? Who says? Why? How?*

Keep checking yourself in this way and the end product will be much more likely to communicate effectively. Questioning like this makes you focus on the key points of what you're writing. It helps to reveal the information that you may take for granted but your audience needs to know, and guides you in where to go next.

Vary the Sentence Length

Anything repeated can become dull. This is true about sentence length. Sentences that are the same length get boring. There is no variety for the reader. The writing lacks any sense of rhythm. It does not sound comfortable. It does not have the patterns of speech. The reader quickly loses interest. See. You're thinking about ducking out for a quick walk to wake you up, or maybe you've started wondering what you're going to have for dinner tonight.

It's useful to vary the length of your sentences. Alternate between long and short sentences. If you have a string of long sentences, you can create more variety by cutting out wordy and repetitive phrases. You can also break some into shorter sentences. Be aware, however, that too many short sentences in a row can make your writing sound jerky and disconnected.

Use long sentences where you need to convey a lot of information or you want to describe something in detail. Use short sentences to make important points.

Vary the Sentence Type

Most sentences follow a basic pattern. Information is presented in the same order, so the reader isn't given much variety. Writers who become stuck in this pattern need to shake things up a little. Sometimes, it's useful to start with an introductory word before the main idea. (Did you notice the introductory word in the last sentence?) Shifting the order of the words around can be useful too. (If that sentence had been *It's also useful to shift the order of the words around,* there would have been less variety of sentence type and you might be snoring by now.)

Your writing can become dull if too many sentences begin with the same word. This is really noticeable with names and such words as *this, the, it* and *I.* If you find this happening, rearrange some sentences to create interest and variety.

End with a Bang

Goodbyes are rarely easy but, to make a lasting impression, it's always important to go out with a bang. Your conclusion should clarify why what you've had to say was important for your audience. They should walk away satisfied by what they've read and glad they took the time to read it (even if they had to).

Good endings often take the reader full circle and go back to echo something that was said in the introduction. Or they point the reader into the future, moving them on to take action or think about something new. Importantly, effective conclusions are brief.

Index

Publisher's Acknowledgements

We're proud of this book; please send us your comments through our online registration form located at `dummies.custhelp.com`.

Some of the people who helped bring this book to market include the following:

Acquisitions, Editorial and Media Development

Project Editor: Charlotte Duff

Acquisitions Editor: Kristen Hammond

Editorial Manager: Alice Berry

Production

Graphics: diacriTech

Proofreader: Jenny Scepanovic

Indexer: Don Jordan, Antipodes Indexing

Screenshot on page 16 © Macquarie School Dictionary, Pan Macmillan Australia

Editorial contributions: Jan Cousens and Erica Michaux (Chapter 12); Diane Furness (Chapter 13); Yasmine McCafferty and Claire Warr (manuscript development).

Every effort has been made to trace the ownership of copyright material. Information that enables the publisher to rectify any error or omission in subsequent editions is welcome. In such cases, please contact the Legal Services section of John Wiley & Sons Australia, Ltd.

Also available . . .

Printed and bound by CPI Group (UK) Ltd, Croydon, CR0 4YY

31/03/2023

03207129-0001